# MOUNTAINEERING IN THE
# SWISS ALPS

## HIGH PEAKS AND CLASSIC CLIMBS IN SWITZERLAND

VERTEBRATE PUBLISHING

**THE AUTHOR**

**Stéphane Maire** is a secondary school teacher with qualifications in electrical engineering and geology. He enjoys every aspect of mountaineering and has climbed extensively in the Mont Blanc range and Eastern Alps. Stéphane's other books include *Alpes valaisannes : Chemins de Lumière*, published by Olizane, *Du Cervin au Léman, Les plus beaux tours du Valais*, published by Glénat, and *Par-delà les Cimes : Sélection d'itinéraires en Suisse*, published by the Swiss Alpine Club. He also contributes to climbing magazines in Switzerland and France.

**ACKNOWLEDGEMENTS**

The pleasures of scaling a large face or traversing a narrow ridge are always greater when they are shared with a trusted companion. I would like to thank all those friends who have had the kindness and patience to accompany me on my trips into the mountains: Laurent, Fred, Serge, Greg, Alex, Dédé, Arnaud, Mathieu, Andrea and David, who, despite his absence, is still with me on all my escapades. Christophe has a special place among these people, as he was my climbing partner on about half the routes included in this guidebook. Even after so many years scrambling in the Alps, he is always up for a long day in the mountains. His unflagging keenness and dependability make him the ideal companion. Thank you, my friend.

**Cover photo:** On the Blüemlisalp Ridge, Bernese Alps.
**Back cover photo:** On the west-east traverse of Liskamm, Valais Alps.

All photography by Stéphane Maire.

First published in 2011 by Éditions Glénat.

Title of the original French edition:
*Alpinisme en Suisse – Grands sommets et courses classiques*
© 2011, Éditions Glénat, 37 rue Servan, 38008 Grenoble, France
'Montagne-Évasion' collection edited by Pascal Sombardier.

This English language edition first published in 2015 in the UK, Europe,
India, South Africa, Australia and New Zealand by Vertebrate Publishing.

Vertebrate Publishing
Crescent House, 228 Psalter Lane, Sheffield S11 8UT, UK.
www.v-publishing.co.uk

All trade enquiries in the UK, Europe and Commonwealth (except Canada) to:
Cordee, 11 Jacknell Road, Dodwells Bridge Industrial Estate, Hinckley, LE10 3BS, UK.
www.cordee.co.uk

Copyright © 2011, Éditions Glénat.

All rights reserved. No part of this work covered by the copyright hereon may be reproduced or used in any form or by any means – graphic, electronic, or mechanised, including photocopying, recording, taping or information storage and retrieval systems – without the written permission of the publisher, authors and editor.

ISBN: 978-1-910240-55-7

Translated from the French by Paul Henderson (traduction@paulhenderson.fr).

Designed and produced by Rod Harrison, Vertebrate Graphics Ltd,
based on an original design by Éditions Glénat. – www.v-graphics.co.uk

Printed in EU by Pulsio SARL.

# MOUNTAINEERING IN THE SWISS ALPS

HIGH PEAKS AND CLASSIC CLIMBS
IN SWITZERLAND

Stéphane Maire
Translated by Paul Henderson

Vertebrate Publishing, Sheffield
www.v-publishing.co.uk

# CONTENTS

| | | |
|---|---|---|
| | Introduction & practical information | 6 |
| | Glossary: English–French–German–Italian | 10 |
| 1 | **Grand Muveran:** Saille Ridge | 12 |
| 2 | **Gastlosen:** South-west–North-east Traverse of the Marchzähne | 14 |
| 3 | **Petit Combin:** North Face | 16 |
| 4 | **Aiguilles Rouges d'Arolla:** North–South Traverse | 18 |
| 5 | **Matterhorn:** Lion Ridge and Hörnli Ridge | 20 |
| 6 | **Besso & Blanc de Moming:** South-west Ridge and Traverse | 24 |
| 7 | **Ober Gabelhorn:** North Face | 26 |
| 8 | **Zinalrothorn:** Rothorngrat and North Ridge | 28 |
| 9 | **Breithorn:** East–West Traverse | 32 |
| 10 | **Liskamm:** West–East Traverse | 36 |
| 11 | **Lenzspitze & Nadelhorn:** North-east Face and Traverse | 38 |
| 12 | **Jegigrat:** South-east Spur of the Grand Gendarme and North-east–South-west Traverse | 40 |

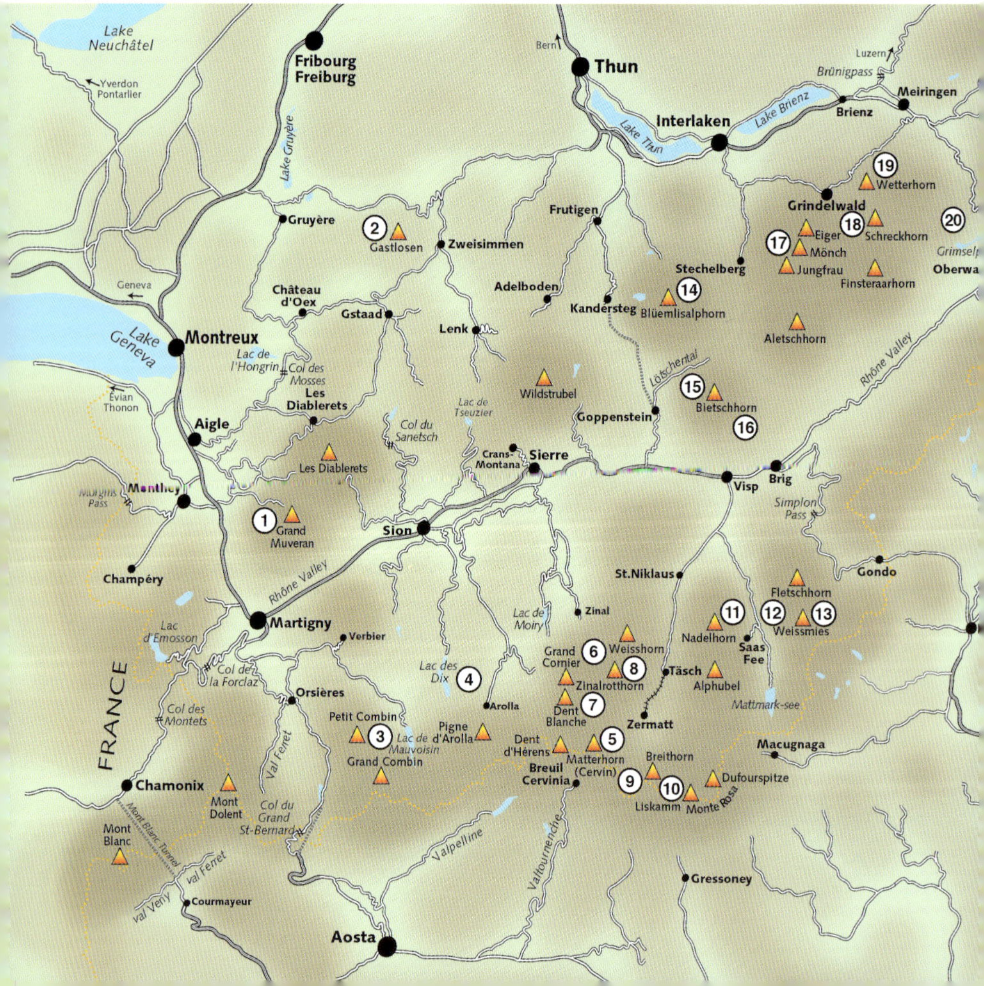

| | | |
|---|---|---|
| 13 | **Weissmies:** North Ridge | 42 |
| 14 | **Blüemlisalphorn & Morgenhorn:** North Face and Traverse of the Ridge | 46 |
| 15 | **Bietschhorn:** East Spur | 48 |
| 16 | **Stockhorn:** South Ridge | 52 |
| 17 | **Mönch:** Nollen | 54 |
| 18 | **Schreckhorn:** South Pillar | 58 |
| 19 | **Klein & Gross Simelistock:** North–South Traverse | 62 |
| 20 | **Gross Diamantstock:** East Ridge | 66 |
| 21 | **Gross Bielenhorn:** South-east Ridge | 68 |
| 22 | **Schijenstock:** South Ridge | 72 |
| 23 | **Salbitschijen:** South Ridge | 74 |
| 24 | **Poncione di Cassina Baggio:** South Ridge | 78 |
| 25 | **Pizzo del Prévat:** North-east Ridge and North-east Pillar | 80 |
| 26 | **Piz Cavardiras:** South Ridge | 82 |
| 27 | **Piz Balzet:** South Ridge | 86 |
| 28 | **Punta da l'Albigna:** Meuli Route | 88 |
| 29 | **Piz Kesch:** North-east Ridge of the Keschnadel and Keschgrat | 92 |
| 30 | **Piz Bernina:** Biancograt | 94 |

# INTRODUCTION

### SMALL COUNTRY, BIG MOUNTAINS

The Swiss Alps have been renowned among climbers ever since travellers began exploring the higher peaks. As the pioneers discovered, Switzerland is an extraordinary playground for mountaineering and offers a huge selection of climbs of all styles and difficulties, spread across the whole country, from the Mont Blanc range in the west to the Bernina mountains in the east.

Set off on a journey across Switzerland and you will quickly see that it is a multi-faceted country, one of whose defining features is its multilingualism. But monoglot visitors need not worry; most Swiss are fluent in more than one of the national languages and many speak excellent English. Sometimes you may not have a language in common, but such occasions just add a little spice to your trip. A foreign holiday would lose much of its exoticism if everyone, even in the most remote valleys of deepest Switzerland, spoke the same language! Hiking up to a hut through unspoilt villages, tasting local specialties, and discovering a valley's traditions and customs are also part of mountaineering, so an open mind is essential if you are to get the most from every outing. For example, you shouldn't come back from the Bernina without having admired the superb houses of the Engadine.

### CHOICE OF ROUTES

Selecting fewer than forty routes to reflect the diversity and quality of climbing in the Swiss Alps is an almost impossible task. Given the huge choice, I could have filled several guidebooks of this size. In fact, if this guidebook is successful, I may put together another collection of climbs, all as good as the routes described here. My initial selection was made in consultation with many other climbers, including mountain guides with wide experience of Switzerland's mountains who were kind enough to send me lists of their favourite routes. The Swiss Alpine Club's comprehensive guidebooks allowed me to expand my choice further. Finally, and this was perhaps the most difficult part of writing this book, I had to reduce the selection to around three-dozen climbs, spread more-or-less equitably across the main climbing areas and including all the different facets of mountaineering, from snow, rock and mixed routes to large north faces, ridge climbs and traverses. Thus, in the final list, world-famous peaks rub shoulders with lesser-known summits, while some classic climbs have been omitted to make way for rarely trodden routes. The selection includes mountains of every stature, from sub-2,000-metre peaks in the Pre-Alps to prestigious 4,000-metre summits in the High Alps, where the rarefied air adds to the difficulties of the climbing. Some outings involve a long walk in to a hut, followed by a climb that will test your stamina. Others can be done in a single day and some are even short enough to be combined with a second route. As a result, this guidebook truly reflects the variety that the Swiss Alps has to offer 'lovers of the heights'. I hope you get as much pleasure out of climbing these routes as I did from preparing this book. Happy climbing.

Under the seracs on the north face of the Petit Combin.

Essential publications.

Near the top of the north face of the Blüemlisalp.

An icon and its admirers in autumn garb.

# PRACTICAL INFORMATION

## HOW TO USE THIS GUIDE
Every chapter begins with a summary of the following practical information:

## ROAD ACCESS
Brief directions are given for people travelling in private cars. These directions are designed to be used in conjunction with a good road map. The relevant 1:25,000-scale map may also be needed to pinpoint the start of the walk in to the hut or the climb. Detailed driving itineraries can be obtained from a number of websites, including **www.viamichelin.com**.

Users of Swiss motorways must buy a toll sticker, which costs CHF 40 and covers the whole country for a year.

If you do not have or prefer not to use a car, the routes in this guidebook can be reached on Switzerland's outstanding public transport network. This takes a little more planning, but the environmental and financial benefits offset the extra effort required. Train and bus times can be obtained in English from **www.cff.ch**. The Swiss Alpine Club website – **www.alpesonline.ch** – combines information about mountain huts, timetables for public transport in the mountains and railway timetables, but this information is not available in English. Information about lifts can be found by typing the name of the lift into any internet search engine.

Half-price travel on trains, post buses and many ski lifts can be obtained by buying a travel pass from the Swiss railway company – **tinyurl.com/half-fare-travelcard**. A year's pass cost CHF 175 in 2015. Visitors intending to travel widely within Switzerland will quickly recoup their investment, especially if they spend time in a resort such as Zermatt, Saas or Grindelwald.

## START POINT
The name of the hut is followed by its altitude, its coordinates on the Swiss 1:25,000-scale map and its telephone number.

To call Switzerland from abroad, replace the 0 of the area code with +41. Swiss telephone numbers have ten digits, including the 0XX area code.

The time required to walk in to the hut is given together with a succinct description of the route to be used in conjunction with the map. Some huts and bivouac shelters are not staffed, or are staffed only at certain times of the year. Even when they are not staffed, all but a few huts provide cooking facilities and some form of heating. Do not forget to pay the hut fees to cover the costs of wood or gas. The policy of the Swiss Alpine Club (CAS) is to keep their huts open to all throughout the year. It would be a shame if the thoughtlessness of a few selfish people were to put that in jeopardy for future generations of climbers.

## DIFFICULTY
Routes are rated using a 'double-entry' system, consisting of an overall grade plus the angle of snow/ice slopes and/or a technical rock-climbing grade (French grades). This section also mentions any potential objective dangers.

## TIMES
Times are given from the hut to the summit and from the summit back to the hut. Sometimes, it can be a long walk from the hut back to the car park and this should be taken into account when planning your trip. All times are given for a team of fit climbers who are well acclimatised (especially important for summits above 4,000 metres) and who climb efficiently (ropework, etc.). These times should be viewed as minimum times.

## VERTICAL HEIGHT
This is the total height climbed between the foot of the route and the summit. Some variation is possible, especially on ridge climbs, but most descents encountered on the route are taken into account.

## CONDITIONS
Only very general information is given here. More detailed information on conditions can be obtained from the hut warden or the local guides office.

## SPECIFIC GEAR
This includes the length of rope required, as well as specific technical gear needed for the route.

Most glacier climbs can be done using a 30-metre rope, if conditions are good (route climbed moving together without taking belays) and if there are no abseils requiring longer ropes.

The gear required for every route – helmet, harness, crevasse-rescue gear (if the route crosses a glacier), first-aid kit, navigation equipment, slings, accessory cord, karabiners – is not listed. The additional gear listed for each route should allow you to cope with most of the situations you are likely to meet; however, this list is purely indicative. For example, you may not need ice screws for a glacier climb if the snow conditions are good.

Given the variations between different brands of cams, cam sizes are given with respect to three widths of cracks, referred to as small (15–30mm), medium (30–60mm) and large (60–80mm). Although most people wear rock shoes on pitches harder than grade 4, it is up to each climber to decide whether or not to use them. Sometimes it is difficult to choose between making the climbing easier and carrying a heavier pack. Recommendations on whether or not to use rock shoes take into account these criteria.

## IN SITU GEAR
Not all rock climbs have been bolted. The *in situ* gear often gives an idea of the type of route and the commitment it requires. It is not unusual to have to replace abseil slings on some of the less popular climbs. A few metres of accessory cord at the bottom of your rucksack can sometimes come in very useful.

## MAPS
This section gives the number and name of the Swiss 1:25,000-scale map(s) covering the area. The relevant 1:50,000 map may be useful for areas that are on the boundary between two larger-scale maps.

## FIRST ASCENT
So we don't forget to whom we owe the wonderful adventure we are about to enjoy.

## ROUTE DESCRIPTIONS
When necessary for the sake of clarity, the approach, climb and descent are described separately.

Only more complex sections of the route and essential changes in direction etc. are described in detail, whereas obvious sections are outlined more succinctly. The objective is to provide enough detail to facilitate route finding without giving a step-by-step description.

Directional terms (left, right, etc.) are always given facing the direction of travel. The terms 'right bank' and 'left bank' are used in their orographic sense.

## PHOTO DIAGRAMS & TOPOS
Every chapter includes a photo, generally taken from the hut or a point on the approach, showing the general line of ascent and descent, including abseils. More detailed topos are given for the rock climbs.

| | |
|---|---|
| Line of the route | ▬ ▬ ▬ ▬ ▬ |
| Variant | • • • • • • • |
| Hidden section | ▬▬▬▬▬▬▬ |
| Abseil ↓    Hidden abseil ↓ | Start of the route: **A** |

## RESCUE
In the case of an accident, the telephone number for the Swiss mountain rescue service (REGA) is 1414 (radio frequency 161.300 Mhz). If you are in the Valais canton, call Air-Glaciers on 1415.

Although mobile phone coverage in the Swiss Alps is quite good, there are still areas where there is no signal. A radio provides the best guarantee of being able to contact the rescue services. Rescue in Switzerland is financed by a donation system. If you are not a Swiss citizen and do not have mountaineering insurance, the cheapest way to get coverage is to become a REGA donor – **www.rega.ch**

## WEATHER
Via internet: **www.meteosuisse.ch**

By telephone: dial 192 or, for a personalised weather report from a Meteosuisse forecaster, dial 0900 162 666 (expensive but very reliable).

# GLOSSARY

| ENGLISH | FRENCH | GERMAN | ITALIAN |
|---|---|---|---|
| **WEATHER** | | | |
| cloudy | nuageux | Wolkig | nuvoloso |
| cold | froid | Kalt | freddo |
| dry | sec | trocken | asciutto, secco |
| fog | brouillard | Nebel | nebbia |
| forecast | prévisions | Wettervorhersage | previsioni |
| hot | chaud | Warm | caldo |
| night | nuit | Nacht | notte |
| rain | pluie | Regen | pioggia |
| storm | orage, tempête | Gewitter, Sturm | temporale |
| sun | soleil | Sonne | sole |
| wind | vent | Wind | vento |
| **GEAR** | | | |
| accessory cord | cordelette | Reepschnur | cordino |
| aid, aid climbing | artificiel, en artif | künstliche Kletterei | arrampicata artificiale |
| altimeter | altimètre | Höhenmesser | altimetro |
| anchor | ancrage, point | Verankerung, Anker | ancoraggio, punto |
| bolt | gollot, spit | Bohrhaken | chiodo a pressione, spit |
| bolt hanger | plaquette | Sicherungsvorrichtung | placchetta |
| broken | cassé | gebrochen, kaput | rotto |
| chain | chaîne | Kette | catena |
| climbing shoes | chaussons d'escalade | Kletterschuhe | scarpette |
| compass | boussole | Kompaß | bussola |
| crampons | crampons | Steigeisen | ramponi |
| expansion bolt | piton à expansion | Bohrhaken | chiodo ad espansione |
| gas cartridge | cartouche de gaz | Gaskartusche | cartuccia di gas |
| gas stove | réchaud à gaz | Gaskocher | fornello a gas |
| gear | équipement, matos | Ausrüstung, Material | materiale |
| glasses | lunettes | Brille | occhiali |
| gloves | gants | Handschuhe | guanti |
| head torch | lampe frontale | Stirnlampe | lampada frontale |
| helmet | casque | Helm | casco |
| hexentric | hexentric | Hexentric, keil | eccentrico |
| ice axe | piolet | Pickel, Eispickel | piccozza |
| ice screw | broche à glace | Eisschraube | chiodo da ghiaccio |
| karabiner | mousqueton | Karabiner | moschettone |
| mountaineering boots | chaussures de montagne | Bergschuhe | scarponi da montagna |
| nut | coinceur | Klemmkeil | nut, dado |
| peg | piton | Haken | chiodo |
| quickdraw | dégaine | Express (schlinge) | rinvio |
| rope | corde | Seil | corda |
| single rope | corde à simple | Einfachseil | corda singola |
| sling | sangle | Bandschlinge | fettuccia |
| sun cream | crème solaire | Sonnencreme | crema solare |
| tent | tente | Zelt | tenda |
| twin rope | corde jumelée | Zwillingsseil | corda gemellare |
| **NAVIGATION – MAPS – GUIDEBOOKS** | | | |
| abseil | rappel | Abseilen | discesa in doppia, calata |
| abseil line | ligne de rappels | Abseilroute | linea di doppie |
| access | accès | Zugang | accesso |
| altitude | altitude | Höhe, Höhenpunkt | quota, altezza |
| bank | rive | Ufer | riva, sponda |
| belay | relais | Stand | sosta |
| bergschrund | rimaye | Bergschrund | crepaccia terminale |
| big | grand | gross | grande |
| bivouac | bivouac | Biwak | bivacco |
| block | bloc | Block | blocco |
| bold | engagé | engagiert | impegnativo |
| bolted | équipé | abgesichert | attrezzato |
| border | frontière | Grenze | confine |
| boulder | bloc de rocher | Felsblock | masso di roccia |
| bridge | pont | Brücke | ponte |
| bulge | bombement | Wulst | pancia |
| cable car | téléphérique | Seilbahn | funivia |
| cairn | cairn | Steinmann | ometto |
| campsite | camping | camping | campeggio |
| car park | parking | Parkplatz | parcheggio |
| chairlift | télésiège | Sessellift | seggiovia |
| chimney | cheminée | Kamin | camino |
| cliff height | hauteur de la paroi | Wandhöhe | altezza della parete |
| climb | montée, ascension | Aufstieg | salita |
| climb (to) | grimper, escalader | klettern | arrampicare |
| climbing | grimpe, escalade | Klettereì | arrampicata |
| combe | combe | Mulde | conca |
| corner | dièdre | Verschneidung, Winkel | diedro |
| cornice | corniche | Wächte | cornice di neve |
| couloir, gully | couloir | Rinne | canale, canalone, gola |
| crack | fissure | Spalt, Riss | fessura |
| crest | crête, arête | Kamm (Berg-), Grat | cresta |
| crevasse | crevasse | Gletscherspalte | crepaccia |

| ENGLISH | FRENCH |
|---|---|
| crux | passage clé |
| dam | barrage |
| danger | danger |
| dangerous | dangereux |
| descend | descendre |
| descent | descente |
| detached block | bloc détaché |
| difficult | difficile |
| difficulty | difficulté |
| direction | direction |
| down-climb | désescalader |
| drag lift | téléski |
| east | est |
| easy | facile |
| escape route | échappatoire |
| exit | sortie |
| exposed | exposé |
| face | versant |
| firm snow | névé |
| flake | écaille |
| forest | forêt |
| fresh snow | neige fraîche |
| glacier | glacier |
| gondola lift | télécabine |
| grade, rating | cotation |
| guide | guide |
| height gain | dénivellation |
| hold | prise |
| hole | trou |
| horizontal | horizontal |
| hut | cabane, chalet, refuge |
| ice | glace |
| icefall | chute de séracs |
| ice wall | paroi de glace |
| icy | verglacé |
| jammed block | bloc coincé |
| laborious | pénible |
| lake | lac |
| ledge | vire |
| left | gauche |
| limestone | calcaire |
| line of the route | trace |
| loose (rock) | délité, friable, pourri |
| main | principal |
| map | carte |
| mixed | mixte |
| moraine | moraine |
| mountain | montagne |
| name | nom |
| narrow | étroit |
| navigation | orientation |
| needle, pinnacle | aiguille, pinacle |
| niche | niche |
| north | nord |
| north side | côté nord |
| notch | brèche |
| obligatory | obligatoire |
| obvious | évident |
| on the left | à gauche |
| on the right | à droite |
| overhang | surplomb |
| pass, saddle | col, selle |
| path, track | sentier, chemin |
| pillar, spur | pilier, éperon |
| pinnacle | gendarme |
| quite difficult | assez difficile |
| quite easy | peu difficile |
| ramp | rampe |
| ridge, arête | arête |
| right | droite |
| river | rivière, fleuve |
| road | route |
| rock | roche, rocher |
| rock wall | paroi rocheuse |
| roof | toit |
| route | itinéraire, voie |
| saddle | selle |
| scree | éboulis |
| scree slope | pierrier |
| section (of a climb) | passage |
| serac | sérac |

10

| GERMAN | ITALIAN | ENGLISH | FRENCH | GERMAN | ITALIAN |
|---|---|---|---|---|---|
| Schlüsselstelle | passaggio chiave | shoulder | épaule | Schulter | spalla |
| Staumauer | diga di sbarramento | signposting | balisage | Markierung | bollinatura, segnaletica |
| Gefahr | pericolo | slab | dalle | Platte | placca |
| gefährlich | pericoloso | sling | anneau de corde, sangle | Schlinge | anello di corda, settuccia |
| absteigen | scendere | slope | pente | Neigung | pendio |
| Abfahrt | discesa | small | petit | klein | piccolo |
| loser block | blocco staccato | smooth | lisse | glatt | liscio |
| schwierig | difficile | snowy ridge | arête de neige | Schneegrat | cresta di neve |
| Schwierigkeit | difficoltà | spur | éperon | Sporn | sperone |
| Richtung | direzione | start | début | Anfang | inizio |
| Abklettern | scendere in arrampicata | start (of a route) | attaque | Einstieg | attacco, inizio della scalata |
| skilift | sciovia | step | ressaut | Aufschwung | risalto |
| Osten | est | stone | pierre, caillou | Stein, Felsen | sasso, pietra |
| leicht, einfach | facile | stone fall | chute de pierres | Steinschlag | caduta di sassi |
| Fluchtweg | scappatoia | stream | ruisseau, torrent | Bach, Wildbach | ruscello, torrente |
| Ausstieg | uscita | strenuous | athlétique | anstrengend | atletico |
| ausgesetzt | esposto | subsidiary summit | antécime | Vorgipfel | anticima |
| Seite | versante | summit | sommet, pointe | Gipfel, Spitze | cima, vetta, punta |
| Firn | nevaio | summit ridge | arête du sommet | Gipfelgrat | cresta della vetta |
| Splitter, Schuppe | scaglia | terrace | terrasse | Absatz, Terrasse | terrazza, terrazzino |
| Wald | bosco | thread | lunule | Sanduhr | clessidra |
| Neuschnee | neve fresca | tooth | dent | Zahn, Horn | dente |
| Gletscher | ghiacciaio | topo | topo | topo | guida topografica |
| Kabinenbahn | cabinovia | tower | tour, gendarme | Turm, Felsturm | torre, gendarme |
| Schwierigkeitsgrad | grado di difficoltà, livello | track | chemin | Fußweg | sentiero |
| Führer | guida | traverse | traversée | Überschreitung, Querung | traversata |
| Höhenunterschied | dislivello | upper | supérieur | obere | superiore |
| Griff | presa | valley | vallée, val | Tal | val, valle |
| Loch | buco | vertical | vertical | senkrecht | verticale |
| waagerecht | orizzontale | very | très, beaucoup | sehr | molto |
| Hütte | capanna, baita, rifugio | very difficult | très difficile | sehr schwierig | molto difficile |
| Eis | ghiaccio | village | village | Dorf | villaggio |
| Eisfall | caduta di seracchi | walk-in | marche d'approche | Anmarsch | avvicinamento |
| Eiswand | parete di ghiaccio | wall | mur, paroi | Wand | muro, parete |
| vereist | ghiacciato | water | eau | Wasser | acqua |
| Klemmblock | masso incastrato | waymarked | balisé | markiert | segnato |
| mühsam | faticoso | west | ouest | West | ovest |
| See | lago | wet | mouillé | nass | bagnato |
| Band, Kante | cengia | | | | |
| links | sinistra | **ACCIDENT – SECOURS** | | | |
| Kalk | calcare | accident | accident | Unfall | incidente |
| Spur | traccia | alarm signal | signal d'alarme | Notsignal | segnale di soccorso |
| morsch, brüchig | friabile, marcio | altitude sickness | mal de montagne | Bergkrankheit | mal di montagna |
| haupt | principale | avalanche | avalanche | Lawine | valanga |
| Landkarte, Karte | carta geografica | broken | cassé | gebrochen, kaput | rotto |
| Fels und Eis | misto | doctor | médecin | Arzt | dottore |
| Moräne | morena | fall | chute | Absturz, Sturz | caduta |
| Gebirge, Berge | montagna | helicopter | hélicoptère | Hubschrauber | elicottero |
| Name | nome | injury | blessure | Verletzung | ferita |
| eng | stretto | mountain rescue | secours en montagne | Bergrettung | soccorso alpino |
| Orientierung | orientamento | radio | radio | Funk | radio |
| Nadel | ago, guglia | radio-telephone | radiotéléphone | Funktelefon | radiotelefono |
| Nische | nicchia | rescue | secours | Hilfe | soccorso |
| Norden | nord | stone fall | chute de pierres | Steinschlag | caduta di sassi |
| Nordseite | versante nord | | | | |
| Scharte, Einschnitt | forcella | **IN THE HUT** | | | |
| obligatorisch | obbligatorio | dormitory | dortoir | Matratzenlager, Schlafraum | dormitorio |
| auffällig | evidente | reserved | réservé | reserviert | prenotato |
| links | a sinistra | tea | thé | Tee | tè |
| rechts | a destra | thirst | soif | Durst | sete |
| Überhang | strapiombo | winter room | refuge d'hiver | Winterraum | rifugio invernale |
| Paß, Joch, Sattel | colle, passo, sella | | | | |
| Pfad, Fussweg, Weg | sentiero | **MOUNTAINEERING TERMS/TECHNIQUES** | | | |
| Pfeiler | pilastro, sperone | (rope) team | cordée | Seilschaft | cordata |
| Gratturm | gendarme | belay | relais | Standplatz | sosta |
| ziemlich schwierig | abbastanza difficile | belaying | assurage | Sicherung | assicurazione |
| mäßig schwierig | poco difficile | climb | ascension | Begehung, Ersteigung | ascensione |
| Rampe | rampa | climber | grimpeur | Kletterer | arrampicatore, scalatore |
| Kante, Grat | spigolo | climbing partner | compagnon de cordée | Partner | compagno di cordata |
| rechts | destra | free climbing | escalade libre | Freiklettern | arrampicata libera |
| Fluss | fiume | guide | guide | Bergführer | guida alpina |
| Straße, Weg | strada | hiker | randonneur | Wanderer | escursionista |
| Gestein, Felsen, Fels | roccia | mountaineer | alpiniste | Bergsteiger | alpinista |
| Felswand | parete rocciosa | pitch | longueur (de corde) | Länge, Seillänge (SL) | lunghezza, tiro di corda |
| Dach | tetto | route | course en montagne | Bergtour | ascensione |
| Route | itinerario, via | sport climbing | escalade sportive | Sportklettern | arrampicata sportiva |
| Einsenkung | sella | two-person team | cordée de deux | Zweierseilschaft | cordata di due |
| Geröll | detriti | | | | |
| Schutthalde | pietraia | **MISCELLANEOUS** | | | |
| Durchgang | passaggio | banned | interdit | Verboten | vietato |
| Gletscherbruch | seracco | be careful | attention ! | Achtung ! | attenzione ! |
| | | identity card | carte d'identité | Ausweis | carta d'identità |

# GRAND MUVERAN (3,051M)

## SAILLE RIDGE
**ROAD ACCESS:** A9 motorway to Riddes, then minor road to Leytron and Ovronnaz.
**START POINT:** Rambert Hut, 2,582m (576'510/119'910). Tel: 027 2071122. 2¼ hrs from the top of the Ovronnaz–Bougnone chairlift.
**DIFFICULTY:** D+, 5b. Quite sustained climbing on the steep part of the ridge but with abundant *in situ* gear. More alpine after that. Complex route finding on the descent.
**TIMES:** approach 30 mins; climb 4–4½ hrs; descent 1 hr.
**VERTICAL HEIGHT:** 580m.
**CONDITIONS:** dry rock. Even a thin layer of snow can make route finding difficult on the descent.
**SPECIFIC GEAR:** 50m rope, rock shoes, eight quickdraws. Approach shoes for the walk in and walk out.
**IN SITU GEAR:** bolts and pegs.
**MAP:** 1305 Dent de Morcles.
**FIRST ASCENT:** Roger Chevalley & Mario Francey, 1937.

Seen from the shores of Lake Geneva, the Grand Muveran fills a wide swathe of the Alpine horizon. Like most of the summits in the limestone Alps, the rock here is generally too poor to give enjoyable climbing, but there is one fabulous exception to this rule – the Saille Ridge. In fact, you have to search far and wide to find a better route on this type of terrain and, since it was rebolted in the 1990s, it has become one of the area's most popular climbs. Superb and sometimes incredibly exposed climbing on the steep initial section leads to an airy traverse along a razor-sharp ridge with a 360° view that takes in the giants of the Valais and Mont Blanc to the south, the Pre-Alps and Lake Geneva to the north, and the Jura Mountains to the west. It would be hard to find a better place from which to brush up on your geography of western Switzerland! What is more, the Saille Ridge's moderate altitude and southerly aspect make it an excellent objective when conditions preclude climbing on higher summits. The second time we did the route, we met an old Chamonix guide with a group from the ENSA guides' school. A good recommendation? We'll let you decide.

### APPROACH
A more or less horizontal path leads from the hut to the saddle at 2,584m, at the foot of the ridge (ask the hut warden to point out the start of the path).

On the final ridge with the summit in sight.

## SAILLE RIDGE
**P0:** A pitch of scrambling leads to the first belay at the start of the difficulties. There is only one hard move (grade 3) and it is protected by a bolt, so it is possible to short-rope this section.
**P1:** Trend right up quite steep ground (4c). Several stepped ledges.
  Walk across to the foot of the next wall (about 10–15m).
**P2:** Either go straight up (strenuous 6a or A0, protected by bolts and pegs) or climb the 5b corner to the left of the wall (also bolted).
**P3:** Superb pitch, 5b. Follow the bolts leftwards. Towards the top, move right round the back of the ridge. Belay before the traverse right.
**P4:** Traverse right, then go straight up. Belay at the end of the difficulties (the next section is very loose, so a trailing rope is likely to knock rocks down). Move together across the scree, staying

# VAUD ALPS

10–15m to the right of the ridge. There is a belay (two bolts) on the right, a little further up the scree, above an island of rock.

P5: Scree at first, then corner-chimney rightwards (3c, bolts and peg). Can be climbed moving together. Care required (stone fall). Belay at the foot of the large step.

P6: Very exposed, well protected (bolts and pegs), 5b.

P7: Layback start (5b – bolt and wooden wedge in the crack). Belay at the top of the step.

## TRAVERSE OF THE RIDGE

Follow the ridge, sometimes along the crest of superb slabs. The first step is tackled directly (bolt and peg), belay at the top. After a long slab, go right round a tower.

## DESCENT

Follow the path down the south face (faded waymarkers, cairns) to the hut. Chimney to downclimb towards the bottom of the face (grade 2).

The crux pitch: excellent climbing in a very exposed position.

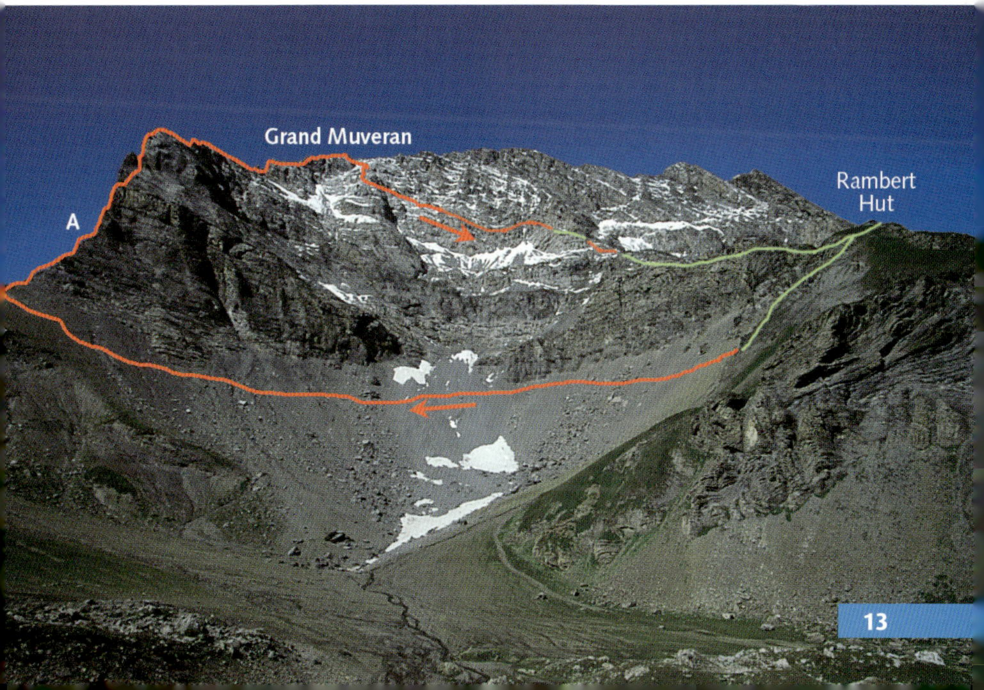

# GASTLOSEN (1,995M)

## SOUTH-WEST–NORTH-EAST TRAVERSE OF THE MARCHZÄHNE

**ROAD ACCESS:** A1 or A9 motorway to Vevey, then A12 to Bulle. From Bulle, go through Broc and Charmey to Jaun. Turn off for Abländschen, just after Jaun.
**START POINT:** the route can be done in a day from the car park at Oberberg. From Jaun, follow the Abländschen road for about 4km. Turn right at spot height 1,134m (sign to *Grat*). Pay the CHF 10 fee to park at Chalet de Mosera, 350m further up the road. Follow the *Chalet Grat* signs and park after crossing the Büelsgrabe stream for the second time (approx. 1,480m). Grids over the drains allow you to park on the left-hand side of the road.
**DIFFICULTY:** D, 5c (4c obligatory). Do not let yourself be led astray by the bolts on the harder traverse (6b) – usually, you will soon realise the climbing has become much more difficult. Carefully inspecting subsequent sections from above will prevent you having to search around for the right ledge or path to follow.
**TIMES:** approach 45 mins; climb 4½–7 hrs; descent 45 mins.
**VERTICAL HEIGHT:** approx. 700m.
**CONDITIONS:** dry rock. Allow the route to dry after rain, as some sections are very slippery in the wet.
**SPECIFIC GEAR:** 50m rope, ten quickdraws, nuts 5 to 9. Rock shoes not essential.
**IN SITU GEAR:** ring bolts for the belays, a few bolts and pegs protect the more difficult sections.
**MAP:** 1226 Boltigen.
**FIRST ASCENT:** Daniel Chervet, W. Richardet & W. Siegfried, 7 September 1924.

The classic traverse of Gastlosen is the only route in the Pre-Alps included in this guidebook, but no one would dispute its place among Switzerland's greatest climbs. First, thanks to its low altitude, the cliff has a very bucolic atmosphere, with spruce forests and Alpine flowers lining the approach, and Fribourg cows grazing contentedly in the lush pastures on either side of the ridge. The chiming of their bells will accompany you all along the route. Second, the ridge's position on the northern edge of the Alps makes it an unrivalled vantage point from which to admire the Bernese Oberland, Vaud Alps, Mont Blanc and the Swiss Plateau. Finally, the climbing on this superb limestone cliff is good enough to satisfy even the most demanding crag rat. Once you have traversed the ridge and got to know the area a little better, you will almost certainly be tempted to come back and do some of the long routes on its south face. Whichever one you choose, you are sure to find great climbing.

### APPROACH

Follow the waymarked path from just behind the car park to the Oberbergpass. The upper section of the path is very steep and you will have to use your hands in places.

### TRAVERSE OF THE RIDGE

Climb the left side of the ridge to the first difficulties, then follow the ridge crest (two pitches, 4b and 4c). Continue easily to the next step, which forms the crux. A difficult pitch (5c+ or 4c/A0) leads to the next belay. Move on to the left side of the ridge and climb a chimney, exiting right to follow easy ground to the summit of the Eggturm (1,934m, 4b).

Go down the path (yellow waymarkers) on the east side of the summit to a notch. Move on to the north face to go round the Kleiner and Grosser Daumen. Follow a path along the base of the cliff to the foot of the Katze. Go round the right-hand side of the Katze to the notch between it and the Pyramide. A pleasant 4c pitch can be climbed to get to the summit of the Katze (abseil descent).

Go over the Pyramide (4a, 4b) and descend to the foot of the next wall. Climb a chimney. From here, either climb the back of a large corner (poor climbing) or the middle of the face to the left (4b, more enjoyable, a few bolts and possible to place nuts).

# FRIBOURG ALPS

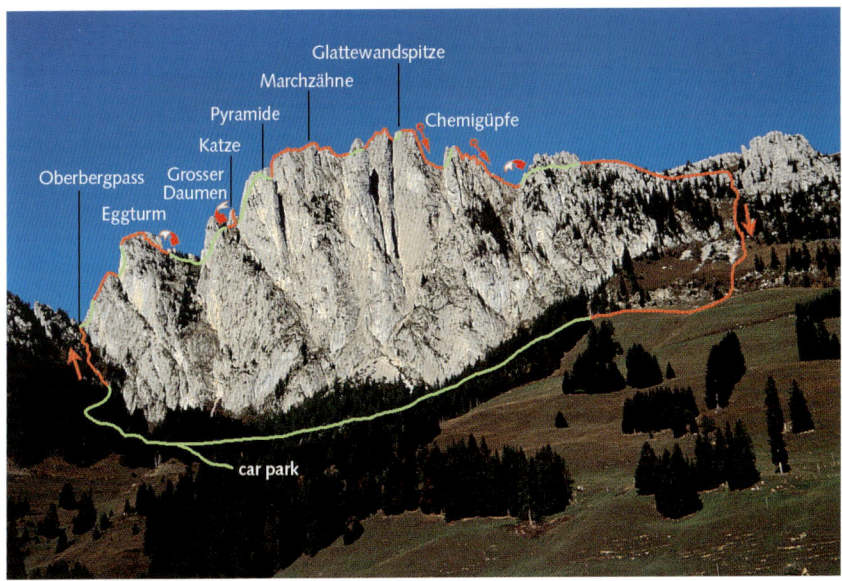

Easily traverse the Marchzähne (2, 3b) and continue to the Glattewandspitze (1,995m, go left round the final step). Do two 20m abseils down the ridge on the left to get to the Glattewandpass. The final tooth on the traverse is the Chemigüpfe (3a, 4c). Climb the left side of the first pinnacle, then abseil back down. The next pinnacle can be climbed on either side (left-hand variant well bolted). Abseil. The final pinnacle can also be climbed on either side. A short abseil leads to two belays (two separate bolts and two bolts with a chain). Go past these belays to another belay, hidden behind a block, a few metres further along the crest of the ridge. Final abseil.

## DESCENT
Follow a faint path, heading left at first then moving back right past wonderful limestone rock formations. Do not descend the gullies on the right, but continue to a shoulder with a distinctive tower. The path leads easily through meadows to the foot of Gastlosen. To get back to the car park, either go straight down to the road or follow the waymarked path (red and white posts) back to the Oberbergpass path followed at the start.

Below the Eggturm, the most difficult tower on the traverse.

# PETIT COMBIN (3,663m)

## NORTH FACE

**ROAD ACCESS:** A9 motorway to Martigny, Grand Saint-Bernard exit. Follow *Grand Saint-Bernard* signs to Sembrancher, then turn left and follow *Verbier* signs to Le Châble. Just after the lights, turn right and follow the Fionnay road to Lourtier. Sign to *Cabane Brunet* just after Lourtier.
**START POINT:** Brunet Hut, 2,103m (587'260/097'660). Tel: 027 7781810 or 079 6284916. Can drive to hut along a good mountain track.
**DIFFICULTY:** AD to D depending on the line taken, 45° or steeper. Difficulty depends greatly on conditions. Long route.
**TIMES:** approach 3 hrs; climb 3–4 hrs; descent 3–4 hrs. The approach can be shortened by bivouacking at Nishliri, 1½ hrs from the hut.
**VERTICAL HEIGHT:** 1,600m.
**CONDITIONS:** face without too many seracs or open crevasses. Best early in the season. Risk of wind slabs after snowfall.
**SPECIFIC GEAR:** 50m rope if you expect steep ice, otherwise 30m is generally sufficient, six to eight ice screws, six quickdraws, crampons, two ice axes each.
**MAPS:** 1326 Rosablanche, 1346 Chanrion.
**FIRST ASCENT:** Denis Bertholet, Hubert Cretton & René Marcoz, as a ski descent, 28 March 1957.

The Combins and their satellites form one of the most beautiful groups of mountains in the Valais Alps. As the only 4,000m peak between the Mont Blanc range and the Dent Blanche, the Grand Combin is the most popular objective for mountaineers in summer. However, several of the monarch's outlying peaks also provide excellent climbs. During a hike in the area, the north face of the Petit Combin grabbed my eye; in fact its rows of seracs and apparent inaccessibility cannot fail to arouse the curiosity of any passing mountaineer. A few months later, with a friend from the Jura, I heeded its siren call. Surrounded by crevasses and hemmed in by seracs, without ever being in real danger, the outcome of our adventure remained uncertain to the very summit – an unexpected luxury on a mountain whose popularity with heli-skiers in winter would suggest it has little to offer in terms of adventure and solitude. But, when summer returns, silence once again shrouds the icy slopes of this exquisite north face, which rarely feels the bite of crampons and ice axe ... Ah, the unknown! One of the face's main attractions is the possibility of varying the difficulty of the ascent to suit your mood, as relatively easy ground is often bounded by steeper slopes requiring greater skill and determination. The choice is yours ...

### APPROACH

From the hut, follow the track to Pindin (2,397m) and then the path to Nishliri (2,492m). Go up the lateral moraine of the Glacier du Petit Combin to around 2,650m. Contour round to the lake below the glacier tongue, then go up the moraine on the left. Continue up the glacier to reach the foot of the face directly below the summit (longitudinal crevasses, best to stay on the left-hand side of the glacier to avoid being under the seracs).

### NORTH FACE

Conditions will dictate the best line to follow.
  There are a few crevasses to cross at the bottom of the face, but the glacier in the middle of the face is much more complex and numerous detours, some quite long, may be needed to avoid the crevasses. In the upper part of the face, it is possible to climb either directly to the summit or to exit on to the north-east ridge.

### DESCENT

Follow the west-north-west ridge (PD), known as the Avagères Ridge, past the Col Est de Lâne (3,037m) to the Col Ouest de Lâne (3,033m). A waymarked descent leads back to the Brunet Hut.

# VALAIS ALPS

**Right:** The upper section of the face seen from the Avagères Ridge.

**Below:** The complex central part of the face.

# AIGUILLES ROUGES D'AROLLA (3,644m)

## NORTH–SOUTH TRAVERSE
**ROAD ACCESS:** A9 motorway to *Sion est*, then Val d'Hérens, Les Haudères, hamlet of La Gouille on the Arolla road.
**START POINT:** Aiguilles Rouges Hut, 2,810m (601'460/100'540). Tel: 027 2831649. 3 hrs from La Gouille via Lac Bleu and Le Remointse du Sex Blanc.
**DIFFICULTY:** AD, 4c (3c obligatory). Rock climb requiring efficient rope work. Numerous climbs and descents. Complex route finding in places.
**TIMES:** approach 1½–2 hrs; traverse 6–7 hrs to the col at 3,624m; descent to La Gouille 2½ hrs.
**VERTICAL HEIGHT:** 1,050m.
**CONDITIONS:** dry rock.
**SPECIFIC GEAR:** 30m rope, four quickdraws, crampons for the approach.
**IN SITU GEAR:** a few pegs.
**MAPS:** 1326 Rosablanche, 1327 Evolène.
**FIRST ASCENT:** M. Chadwick with the guides Bernet and Christian Jossi, 28 June 1897.

Aiguille and traverse: two words that are often associated in the Alps, rarely for the worse, although some people are put off by the numerous ascents and descents this type of climb usually involves. Moving quickly on a route such as the traverse of the Aiguilles Rouges d'Arolla is generally a question of experience and efficient rope work. When conditions are good, the climbing is straightforward, but speed is of paramount importance, as there are few escape routes and getting caught in an afternoon storm would not be fun. However, the rock is good, the climbing over fifteen gendarmes is pleasant, and the setting is magnificent, so climbers used to this sort of terrain are sure to have a great time. There are even a few sections of more difficult climbing to add a little spice to the route. Finally, and somewhat surprisingly, the traverse is rarely crowded, perhaps because most mountaineers head straight to the more famous summits at the head of the Val d'Hérens.

## NORTH–SOUTH TRAVERSE
From the hut, go up the Glacier Supérieur des Aiguilles Rouges to the snowy saddle to the north of the north summit (approx. 3,430m). Go over the north summit (loose rock, stay on the east side of the ridge) to the north col (approx. 3,535m). Traverse a gendarme via its ridge.

Continue past a notch, then traverse right to the rib on the edge of the gully below the central summit. Climb this rib to three-quarters height, then move left back on to the ridge. Traverse 5m across the east face, then follow the crest of the ridge to the central summit (3,646m). Go down a small chimney, then follow the ridge to the saddle between the central and south summits (approx. 3,460m). There are 15 gendarmes (numbered 1 to 15 below) between the saddle and the south summit.

Solid, warm-coloured rock.

# VALAIS ALPS

The traverse includes many sections of pleasant climbing.

Go past no.1, then follow a ledge on the east face, 10m below no.2, to a notch at the foot of no.3 (steep-sided gully above the Glacier Inférieur des Aiguilles Rouges). Gain a hole in the ridge. Stay on the east side to gain the 'cock's comb', a detached blade of rock below no.4. Go past the cock's comb (squeeze between the blade and the wall if you are small enough, otherwise straddle across it). It is also possible to climb no.4 directly (4c). Follow a scree-covered ledge for 15m to a cairn, then go up a lateral ridge to the foot of no.5. Follow a ledge on to the west face, then climb no.5 via a nice, 15m slab (3c, crux if the difficult gendarmes are avoided). Climb no.6 via an overhang and 5m slab on the east face. Traverse no.7 and no.8 via an overhang and a slab on the east face. No.9 is climbed diagonally on the same face. Descend a few metres on the east side of no.10 and climb a wide crack to a scree-covered terrace, then a slab near its summit. No.11 is easy. No.12 is climbed by a wide crack on the east face, no.13 via a short vertical slab. No.14 and no.15 are overcome easily to reach the south summit (3,584m).

## DESCENT

Gain the first gendarme on the south ridge. Descend diagonally across the east face to Col Slingsby (3,498m). Move on to the west face, then descend diagonally across a few gullies to regain the start of the south ridge as quickly as possible. From 50m below the saddle at 3,264m, follow the path to the saddle. Descend eastwards and follow the Col des Ignes path either back to the hut or directly to Lac Bleu.

# MATTERHORN (4,478m)

## LION RIDGE AND HÖRNLI RIDGE

**ROAD ACCESS:** A9 motorway to *Sierre-est*, then Visp, Stalden, Täsch and train to Zermatt.
**START POINT:** Jean-Antoine Carrel Hut, 3,829m (616'210/091'300). Booking not possible. Staffed intermittently in summer. Cooking stoves and gas available, but it is best to take your own cooking kit in high season. PD, 5¾ hrs from Plan Maison via the Duca degli Abruzzi Hut.
**DIFFICULTY:** AD+, 3. The length of the route (especially the descent) and route finding are the main difficulties. Most local guides will be happy to help you stay on route during the descent of the Hörnli Ridge. Offering to buy a helpful guide a beer when you get back to the hut never goes amiss.
**TIMES:** Lion Ridge 4–5 hrs; descent 4–5 hrs. No need to start too early (4 a.m. is early enough), as it is very easy to get off route in the dark and end up on very loose ground where it is almost impossible not to knock stones down on to parties below you.
**VERTICAL HEIGHT:** 645m, descent 1,220m.
**CONDITIONS:** dry rock. Snow is not necessarily a problem but it makes the descent, particularly the section around the Tête du Cervin, more difficult.
**SPECIFIC GEAR:** 30m single rope, crampons, ice axe, four quickdraws.
**IN SITU GEAR:** fixed ropes, rope ladder, iron bars, bolts.
**MAPS:** 1347 Matterhorn, 1348 Zermatt.
**FIRST ASCENT:** Lion Ridge: the guides Jean-Baptiste Bich & Jean-Antoine Carrel, 17 July 1865. Hörnli Ridge: Edward Whymper, D.R. Hadow, Charles Hudson, Francis Douglas, with the guides Michel-Auguste Croz, Peter Taugwalder father & son, 14 July 1865.

The perfect peak? Although the contrast between its elegant silhouette and the indifferent quality of the rock can come as a surprise, the Matterhorn is a truly exceptional mountain. No one arriving in Zermatt for the first time is left unmoved by their first sight of this extraordinary pyramid. Of course, fame also has its disadvantages and it isn't unusual for the Matterhorn's two normal routes to be overrun with climbers. However, by waiting patiently for the right moment, it is possible to avoid the busiest periods. As for the sometimes-poor rock, innumerable ascents by generations of mountaineers have cleaned up the most friable sections – as long as you stay on route – and fixed ropes facilitate progress where the rock remains more doubtful.

Traversing the Matterhorn from Italy to Switzerland (or from Switzerland to Italy, if you want to be in the sun) remains an unforgettable and fulfilling experience that no lover of the high mountains should forego. How many climbers have never dreamt of standing on the summit of this proud icon?

*The Tête du Cervin seen from the end of the Tyndall Ridge*

### APPROACH TO THE JEAN-ANTOINE CARREL HUT

From Zermatt, take the lifts to the Klein Matterhorn. Descend to Testa Grigia (waymarked glacier but climbers should still rope up) and use the Breuil lifts to get to Plan Maison (reached directly from Breuil if you are coming from Italy). Head north to the Duca degli Abruzzi Hut (2,802m). Follow the path to the Croce di Carrel, then head up 'alpine' terrain below the Testa del Leone (fill up water bottles below the last snowfields) and climb the ridge (partly equipped) to the hut (3,829m).

# VALAIS ALPS

5

Above: Looking across to the Matterhorn and Dent d'Hérens.

# MATTERHORN
## LION RIDGE AND HÖRNLI RIDGE

### LION RIDGE
Go up the fixed ropes to the Great Tower, behind the old hut. The next fixed rope leads to the ledge at the top of the Vallon des Glaçons. Traverse right, then climb a corner and slabs to get back on to the ridge. Go round the right-hand side of some pinnacles. Traverse the narrow, slanting ledge of the 'Mauvais Pas' (10m, 3, peg). Gain the snowfield of the 'Linceul' and go up its left edge. Climb the 'Tyndall Rope' (30m of chains), then follow the crest of the ridge (with a few detours on to the north face) to Pic Tyndall (4,241m). Traverse the Tyndall Ridge and cross the 'Enjambée' cleft. Follow the ridge crest to the next ropes before the 'Jordan Ladder'. The last two ropes lead to the Italian summit (4,476m). Descend to the notch, then go up to the Swiss summit (4,478m).

### HÖRNLI RIDGE
Head north-east down the scree-covered ridge, then follow the fixed ropes. Go down the ridge to the Solvay Hut. Some more difficult sections can be avoided, but the route is mostly on the ridge crest or slightly to the right (metal bars and bolts). Descend leftwards below the hut, then go down to the Moseleyplatte (metal bars). At the bottom of this section, bear left, parallel to the ridge, for about 100m to get to the Gebiss (bars). Keep descending, often moving back left (don't go too far on to the east face, metal bars and bolts). Continue down ledges, then a path of yellowish rock that traverses the east face and leads to Auf dem Grat, an obvious tower on the ridge. Don't follow the marks that lead to a gully on the right, instead go over the tower. Descend rightwards, then move back left (fixed rope) to get to a horizontal section of the ridge. Descend to the right of the tower for a short distance to a second gully. Follow the left bank of this gully (stepped ledges) to a ledge. Head rightwards along this ledge to the start of a third gully – the Erstes Couloir (first gully) for climbers coming up the Hörnli Ridge. Go down a chimney and a corner. At the end of the corner, traverse right and descend to the foot of a tower beside the gully on the right. Follow a ledge (faint path) leftwards and go over the gully. Traverse across scree towards the hut. Use the metal bars and fixed rope to descend the final difficult section.

Dent d'Hérens and Dent Blanche, with Mont Blanc in the distance on the far left.

# VALAIS ALPS

Descent via the Hörnli Ridge.

- Matterhorn
- Solvay Hut (emergencies only)
- Auf dem Grat
- Erstes Couloir
- Hörnli Hut

# BESSO (3,667m)
# & BLANC DE MOMING (3,663m)

## SOUTH-WEST RIDGE AND TRAVERSE

**ROAD ACCESS:** A9 motorway to *Sierre-est*, then Val d'Anniviers, Zinal. Car park on the southern edge of the resort.
**START POINT:** Mountet Hut, 2,886m (616'630/100'960). Tel: 027 4751431. 4½ hrs from Zinal via Le Vichiesso and the path above the right bank of the Zinal Glacier.
**DIFFICULTY:** AD+, 4. Beware of stone fall in the approach gully. Descent difficult to follow in poor visibility.
**TIMES:** approach 1–1½ hrs; climb 6½–7 hrs; descent 2 hrs.
**VERTICAL HEIGHT:** 960m
**CONDITIONS:** dry rock, although a little snow shouldn't pose too many problems.
**SPECIFIC GEAR:** 30m rope, four quickdraws. Crampons and ice axe are unnecessary if conditions are very good (i.e. track for the snowy part of the Blanc de Moming. Ask the hut warden.).
**IN SITU GEAR:** a few bolts.
**MAP:** 1327 Evolène.
**FIRST ASCENT:** Sir Henry Seymour King with the guides Aloys Anthamatten and Ambros Supersaxo, 28 July 1886.

The peaks forming the imperial crown that rises above the Mountet Hut, at the head of the Anniviers Valley, need no introduction. Weisshorn, Zinalrothorn, Ober Gabelhorn, Dent Blanche and Grand Cornier, to name just the most famous, are prized objectives for most mountaineers. Although these great peaks often overshadow their smaller neighbours, summits such as the Besso and Blanc de Moming are by no means devoid of charm. First, because they lie in the heart of the sanctuary, they are unrivalled vantage points from which to admire the jewels in Zinal's crown. Then there is the excellent rock, which provides fine climbing protected by judiciously placed bolts in sections that would otherwise be excessively bold. Finally, the short approach and easy descent mean both summits can be climbed in a day. All these qualities should be enough to convince even the most reticent. When crowds are assailing the ridges of the great 4,000ers, it is often quite satisfying to be watching from afar while enjoying an equally beautiful but much more peaceful climb.

### APPROACH
Follow the hut access path back almost to the moraine of the Glacier du Besso. Turn right at a boulder bearing the name *Besso* in red paint (look out for this boulder during the walk in to the hut) and head towards the narrow gully that leads to the south-west ridge of the Besso, about 100m east of spot height 3,217m. Climb the back of the gully (4) or its right bank (easier but loose rock), exiting rightwards at the top to gain the ridge.

Looking along the ridge to the summit of the Besso.

24

# VALAIS ALPS

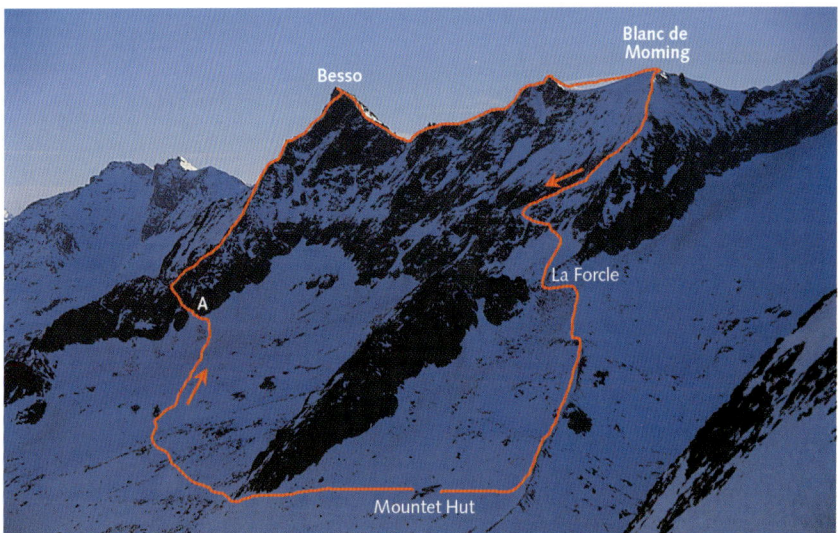

## BESSO: SOUTH-WEST RIDGE
Go over the first gendarmes. Short abseil after the last pinnacle. An easier section of the ridge leads to a large step. Climb a cracked slab (3c), then follow the right-hand side of the ridge (bolt behind the crest) to a chimney. Climb this chimney and go over two more small gendarmes to gain the foot of the summit buttress. Turn this buttress on the right to reach the summit from the south.

## BESSO–BLANC DE MOMING
From the summit, descend the east face (cairn) to gain the south-east ridge at a notch. Go down to the lowest point between the two summits (3,519m), then follow the crest of the ridge to the north summit of Blanc de Moming (a few bolts), turning the gendarmes on the left.

## DESCENT
Go down snow to the Dôme, then head south-west down the ridge. Go past spot height 3,555m. When the ridge becomes steep and loose, head down rightwards to a snowy shoulder at around 3,350m. Bear diagonally leftwards across the south face and follow easy ledges to La Forcle (numerous cairns on the ridge). From La Forcle (3,188m), go down to the moraine and follow the path back to the hut.

Dent Blanche and Grand Cornier.

# OBER GABELHORN (4,063M)

## NORTH FACE
**ROAD ACCESS:** see route no.6 (page 24).
**START POINT:** see route no.6 (page 24).
**DIFFICULTY:** D, 450m at 50/55°. Do not underestimate the approach and descent (steep ground). It is important not to descend too late in order to avoid the risk of stone fall.
**TIMES:** approach 3 hrs; climb 3 hrs; descent 3 hrs.
**VERTICAL HEIGHT:** 1,320m, including the return to the hut.
**CONDITIONS:** snow on the face. The climb will take much longer if there are sections of bare ice. Conditions are usually best in late spring/early summer but the season can be longer if the summer is cool and damp.
**SPECIFIC GEAR:** 50m rope, six to eight ice screws, six quickdraws, two ice axes each, crampons.
**MAP:** 1327 Evolène.
**FIRST ASCENT:** Hans Kiener & Rudolf Schwarzgruber, 30 July 1930.

Is this the purest wall of ice in the Alps? There are steeper, bigger, higher, more famous and more varied faces than this, but none of them are so geometrically perfect. Anyone who appreciates a perfect line cannot fail to be mesmerised by the immaculate whiteness of this snowy triangle pointing towards the heavens. Conditions on this sort of terrain depend mostly on the snow cover. On one ascent I can remember, on 1 August 2000, the steps left by our predecessors were so deep we could have left our crampons at home. A few weeks later, the slope had turned to bare ice, forcing us to climb it in pitches and doubling the time taken. Topping out from the north face is one of the most fantastic summit experiences in the Alps as, all of a sudden, the magical silhouettes of the Matterhorn and the Dent d'Hérens rise up before you.

### APPROACH
From the hut, follow the path south to the Glacier du Mountet. Traverse the glacier tongue to the foot of the Cœur, an island of rock at the foot of the north-west ridge of the Ober Gabelhorn. Go up the snow to the left of the Cœur to gain a large ledge that runs across the entire west face to the north-north-west ridge. If the slope below the ledge is bare ice, climb the rocks just above the Cœur. Continue up snow slopes to the foot of the north face (crevasses).

### NORTH FACE
Cross the bergschrund, then climb the face directly below the summit. Exit rightwards to avoid the loose rock at the summit.

### DESCENT
Follow the snowy crest of the north-west ridge to spot height 3,690m. Move right and go down easy rocks and a steep snow slope to the plateau of the Glacier de l'Obergabelhorn. Follow the approach route back to the hut.

Looking across the top of the face to the Zinalrothorn and the Weisshorn.

26

# VALAIS ALPS

**7**

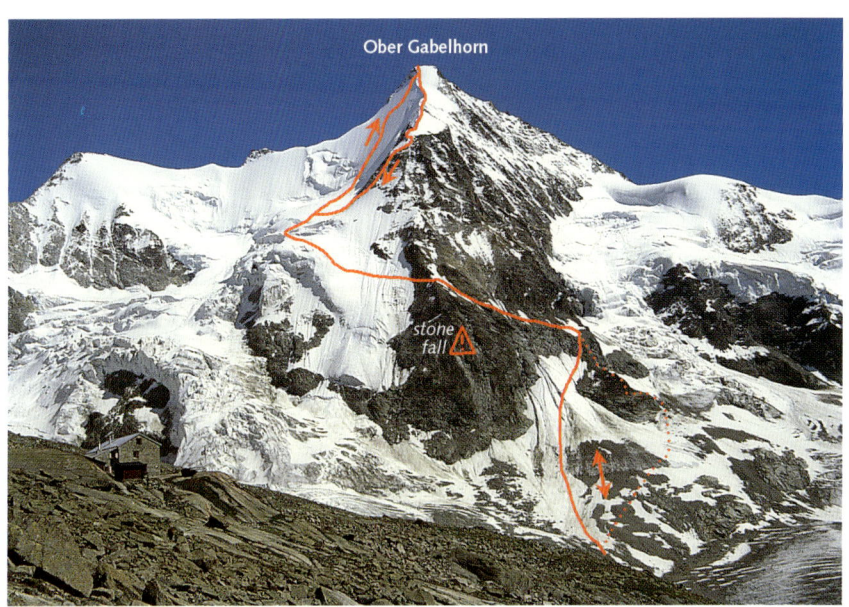

Lines of convergence.

# ZINALROTHORN (4,221m)

## ROTHORNGRAT AND NORTH RIDGE

**ROAD ACCESS:** see route no.6 (page 24).
**START POINT:** see route no.6 (page 24).
**DIFFICULTY:** AD+, 4. Requires a full range of mountaineering skills. Glacier can be difficult to cross. The descent via the Arête du Blanc requires care and energy.
**TIMES:** approach 2½ hrs; climb 3 hrs; descent 3–4 hrs.
**VERTICAL HEIGHT:** 1,350m
**CONDITIONS:** snow on the slope below the Rothornjoch, dry rock on the Rothorngrat, snow on the Arête du Blanc. This combination of conditions is rarely found at the end of the season.
**SPECIFIC GEAR:** 50m single rope, ice axe and crampons, six quickdraws.
**IN SITU GEAR:** a few bolts and pegs.
**MAP:** 1327 Evolène.
**FIRST ASCENTS:** Rothorngrat: C.R. Gross with the guide Rudolf Taugwalder, August 1901. North Ridge: Leslie Stephen, F. Crawford Grove with the guides Melchior & Jakob Anderegg, 22 August 1864.

Excellent rock and magnificent views of the Valais' other great 4,000m peaks have helped the Rothorngrat gain a reputation for being the best ridge climb around Zermatt. Its sharply serrated crest is also extremely distinctive, resembling a series of frozen waves when viewed from the Rothornjoch. The climbing along this razor's edge of rock and snow flows naturally, and there is rarely any hesitation about which way to go, as, rather satisfyingly, the route traverses all the gendarmes.

Once on the summit, the north ridge stretches before you, an irresistible invitation to complete the traverse of this beautiful peak. Ahead, a few more difficulties remain to be overcome before you begin the descent down the vertiginous Arête du Blanc. But even if conditions are good, don't let your mind start wandering too soon, or you could end up finishing the traverse with a breakneck slide down 50° slopes! Back on the glacier, strolling down to the hut, you will have plenty of time to glance round and relive a day that you will already be counting as one of your greatest memories.

During the approach, the Dent Blanche is already in the sun while the north face of the Ober Gabelhorn remains in shadow.

# VALAIS ALPS

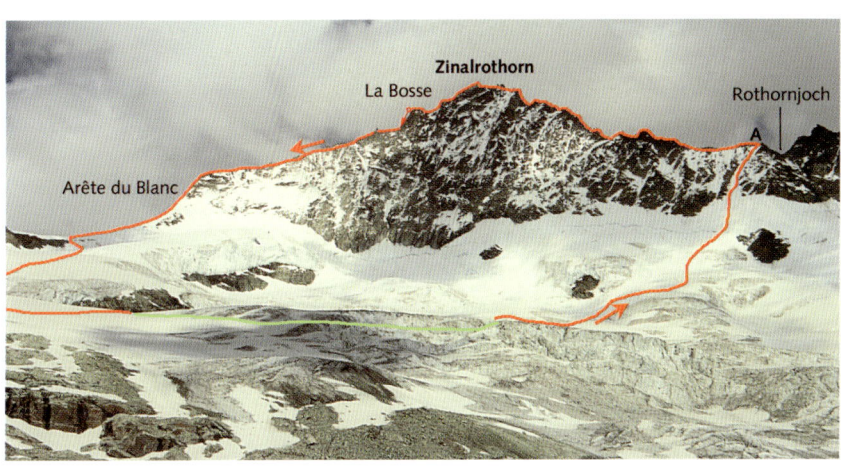

*The sometimes exposed climbing along the north ridge adds interest to the descent.*

# ZINALROTHORN
## ROTHORNGRAT AND NORTH RIDGE

A mountaineer's dream?

### APPROACH
From the hut, follow the path up the moraine to go past La Forcle (3,188m) and gain the Glacier du Mountet at around 3,300m. Cross the glacier to the south of spot height 3,364m, going above or below, depending on conditions, the subsequent area of crevasses. Cross the bergschrund and climb the steep snow slope (ice at the end of the season) to gain the crest of the ridge just north of the Ober Rothornjoch (3,835m).

### SOUTH-WEST RIDGE – ROTHORNGRAT
Climb the ridge above the Rothorngrat, staying as close to the crest as possible. Any difficulties can be avoided by moving on to the Mountet side of the ridge. Climb the second gendarme via a diagonal chimney on its left side (3a), then go left round its summit. Climb the third gendarme directly (3c). All the other gendarmes as far as the Grand Gendarme are climbed directly (4a) or turned on the left (3a). The Grand Gendarme is the last but one pinnacle before the Gabel, the notch where the normal route from Zermatt meets the traverse. For the Grand Gendarme, go up a few metres to a platform (peg), then traverse 1m right and climb a wall (peg) and a short crack (4, bold) to get to another platform. A slab (bolt, 4a) and a short corner lead to the summit. Turn the final, two-pointed pinnacle via a ledge on the west face to get to the Gabel. Follow the ridge crest to a short wall, then move left (peg) to a slab (the Biner-platte). Traverse left across this slab (peg), then move back right on to the crest (3, metal bar and peg). Go right to avoid a final tower (the Kanzel) and reach the summit.

### DESCENT VIA THE NORTH RIDGE
Descend to the first major step in the ridge (the Bosse). Do two abseils (15m and 25m), then continue to a narrow and almost horizontal section of the ridge (the Bourrique), which is traversed either with your hands on the crest or by straddling the crest. Go round the Sphinx via a ledge on the left (bolts), then go over the Rasoir (3). Abseil or climb down from the Rasoir. Go right round the Gendarme du Déjeuner. The ridge becomes easier and quickly leads to the Arête du Blanc (difficult move just before the snow, one peg). Go along the exposed crest of the ridge to spot height 3,732m and the Glacier du Mountet.

Follow the approach route back to the hut.

# VALAIS ALPS

**8**

The view looking back along the Rothorngrat from just below the summit is truly magnificent.

# BREITHORN (4,164m)

## EAST–WEST TRAVERSE
**ROAD ACCESS:** see route no.5 (page 20).
**START POINT:** Klein Matterhorn cable car station, 3,817m. From late June to early September it is possible to do the route in a day by taking the first lift in the morning. Outside this period the first cable car leaves too late. You can also spend the night at the Rossi e Volante bivouac hut (3,787m), below the Roccia Nera. (625'780/086'550). 2 hrs from the Klein Matterhorn station. Six places. Take a stove and gas for cooking.
**DIFFICULTY:** AD+, 4. Very varied route requiring both rock climbing and ice climbing skills. Difficult but easy to protect sections of rock climbing. Cornices. Possible to start at the Breithorn Central if the weather is unsettled. Similarly, if the weather deteriorates, it is quite easy to escape via the south face of the chain.
**TIMES:** approach 2 hrs; traverse 6 hrs.
**VERTICAL HEIGHT:** 750m
**CONDITIONS:** generally in condition all summer. The sections of rock climbing dry quickly after bad weather. Be careful if there is fresh snow on the slopes of the Roccia Nera. The aspect of the ridge means it is best avoided in windy conditions.
**SPECIFIC GEAR:** 50m rope, six quickdraws, crampons, ice axe.
**IN SITU GEAR:** *in situ* belay for the first step of the Breithorn Central and three bolts in each of the two pitches.
**MAP:** 1348 Zermatt.
**FIRST ASCENT:** Eduard Hahn & companions, 19 July 1900.

Monte Rosa has a unique place in the minds of 4,000m-peak baggers, as climbers looking to expand their list of conquests can make an excellent haul in this area in just a few days. However, the climbing is of limited technical interest, often involving hours of walking with only the magnificent scenery to relieve the monotony. In contrast, traversing the neighbouring ridge of the Breithorn allows you to reap five summits above the magic altitude (all UIAA certified!) while climbing a superb route. The variety of the outing, in terms of both the views and the terrain, should satisfy even the most demanding mountaineer. Halfway along the traverse, after a series of elegant snowy arêtes, the rocky spur of the Breithorn Central provides an outstanding pitch of climbing that on its own would make the trip worthwhile. It is probably the best pitch on any of the Valais' 4,000m peaks. In addition, this 2.5km journey between heaven and earth ends by following the easiest normal route on a 4,000m peak back to the Klein Matterhorn station. What more could you want?

A perfect mix of snow and rock.

### EAST–WEST TRAVERSE
From the Klein Matterhorn station, briefly follow the normal route, then bear right to go past the foot of the rock island at 3,831m. Traverse below the south face of the Breithorn chain until directly above the Rossi e Volante bivouac hut. Go up a snow slope to the Roccia Nera, then traverse easily to the gendarme at 4,106m (cornices).

# VALAIS ALPS

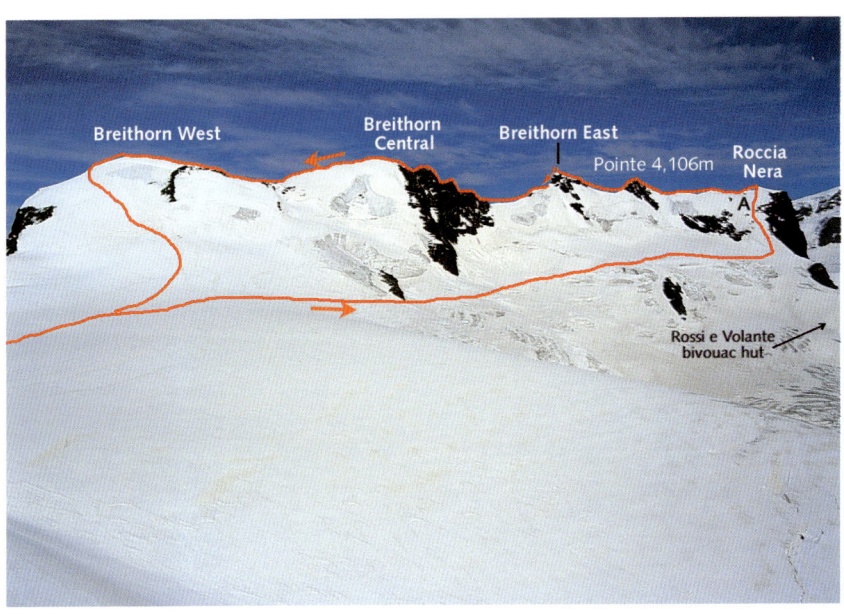

All good things come to an end. Looking back along the ridge to the summits of Monte Rosa.

# BREITHORN
## EAST–WEST TRAVERSE

Descend to the snow (exposed, one peg at half height), then climb the east summit. Descend from the summit via two abseils (25m for the second). Another section of snow leads to the foot of the Breithorn Central.

Follow an easy ledge to the start of the difficulties. Go straight up to a fin of rock that leads leftwards to the foot of the summit step (belay), which is climbed via a magnificent 30m pitch (two bolts). The route is mostly on the right-hand side of the ridge, sometimes on the crest and sometimes just to its right (4c, exposed but easy to protect and on excellent rock). Continue along the crest and climb two final steps. This section of rock climbing can be avoided by going up the gully on the south face, but doing so would be almost criminal. Continue to the central summit (4,159m), following the abundant scratch marks on the rock.

A small gendarme provides a final obstacle (3c, peg) just before the snow. Go along the snowy ridge to the west summit (4,164m), then follow the obvious track of the normal route back to the Klein Matterhorn.

The beauty and variety of this magnificent traverse encapsulated in a single image.

Exposed climbing on the Breithorn Central.

# VALAIS ALPS

# LISKAMM (4,527m)

## WEST–EAST TRAVERSE
**ROAD ACCESS:** from the north, A9 motorway to Martigny, then Grand Saint-Bernard Tunnel (toll) to Aosta. From Aosta, take the motorway to Pont-Saint-Martin, then go up the Gressoney Valley to Stafal. From the south, head to Pont-Saint-Martin, either from Bourg-Saint-Maurice via the Col du Petit-Saint-Bernard, or from Turin via the motorway.
**START POINT:** Quintino Sella Hut, 3,585m (627'450/083'250). Tel: +39 0125366113. 3 hrs from the top of the Stafal–Colle di Bettaforca gondola lift. Buy a combined Bettaforca–Passo dei Salati ticket for the descent.
**DIFFICULTY:** AD, grade-3 rock, 45° snow. Difficulty depends on conditions. Ice on the narrow sections of the ridge can make the traverse much harder. Cornices.
**TIMES:** approach 2 hrs; traverse 3 hrs; descent 3–4 hrs.
**VERTICAL HEIGHT:** 1,150m
**CONDITIONS:** snow on the ridge. Avoid periods when it is very cold and windy. Risk of wind slabs after fresh snowfalls.
**SPECIFIC GEAR:** 30m rope, crampons, ice axe, three ice screws for the rope team, three quickdraws.
**IN SITU GEAR:** an *in situ* sling helps protect the mixed ground between the two summits.
**MAPS:** 1348 Zermatt, and 294 Gressoney (1:50,000).
**FIRST ASCENT:** Edward N. Buxton & Leslie Stephen with the guides Jakob Anderegg & Franz Biner, 16 August 1864.

The 'man-eater' is a very popular mountain, despite its deadly reputation – the cornices lining the giant's ridge have taken a heavy toll on unwary climbers who were too slow to realise the danger of straying too close to the edge of the snow. Even the approach from Switzerland has claimed its share of victims, engulfed by the treacherous ice of the Grenzgletscher. As a result, most people now prefer to start this glorious traverse from Italy. The approach from the south makes the route much easier – as long as the ridge is covered in snow, not ice – giving you more freedom to enjoy the magnificent views. However, there are also sections where you have to remain attentive as you tread the thin line between fragile cornices and precipitous, 50° slopes. When you return from this wonderful climb, your remaining duty is to help restore the honour of a mountain that is truly grand, both in stature and in terms of the glorious spectacle it provides the tourists who have come from Zermatt to admire its vast expanses of ice.

### APPROACH
From the hut, head north along a generally well-marked track (crevasses) to the Felikhorn (4,087m). Cross the plateau to the north-east and climb the south-west ridge of the Liskamm. Towards the top, if conditions are poor, keep on the right-hand side of the ridge (rock for placing runners).

### TRAVERSE
A short descent in the mixed part of the traverse is protected by an *in situ* sling. Go up easily from the Sella del Liskamm (4,417m) to the summit.

### DESCENT
Descend the steep snow slope below the summit, then go down the ridge (very narrow at the bottom), staying just to the left of the crest, to the Lisjoch (4,151m). Follow the track south to the Gnifetti Hut. Continue heading south across the tongue of the Ghiacciaio di Garstelet to a ridge of boulders. Go down to the Ghiacciaio d'Indren (fixed ropes) and gain the top of the Alagna lifts at Punta Indren (approx. 3,250m). The Colle d'Olen path starts below the main building. Follow this path across the west face of the Stolemberg (3,202m). A few sections with fixed ropes lead to the top of the Passo dei Salati gondola lift (2,672m).

# VALAIS ALPS

**Right:** The descent stretches out before you.

**Below:** Strong winds on the crest can force you to your knees.

37

# LENZSPITZE (4,294m)
# & NADELHORN (4,327m)

## NORTH-EAST FACE AND TRAVERSE
**ROAD ACCESS:** A9 motorway to *Sierre-est*, then Visp, Stalden, Saas Fee.
**START POINT:** Mischabel Hut, 3,335m (634'810/106'530). Tel: 027 9571317. 4 hrs from Saas Fee via Schönegge. Numerous hairpins towards the bottom and via ferrata towards the top. Taking the ski lifts to Hannigalp saves an hour.
**DIFFICULTY:** D, 50–55° for the face, AD, 3c for the traverse. Difficulty depends on the amount of snow on the face and the ridge – it is very rare to have optimal conditions on both.
**TIMES:** approach 1½ hrs; North-east Face 3–4 hrs; traverse 2 hrs; descent 2½ hrs.
**VERTICAL HEIGHT:** 1,050m.
**CONDITIONS:** snow on the face. Best in the spring and early summer, but summer snowfall can give good conditions later in the season.
**SPECIFIC GEAR:** 50m rope, six to eight ice screws, six quickdraws, crampons, two ice axes each.
**MAP:** 1328 Randa.
**FIRST ASCENTS:** North-east Face: Dietrich von Bethmann-Hollweg with the guides Oskar & Otmar Supersaxo, 7 July 1911. Traverse: M. von Kuffner & A. Burgener, July 1894.

The North-east Face of the Lenzspitze points up to the sky like a curved mirror, rising 400m from the bergschrund to the summit. When snow conditions are good, the climbing is straightforward and the face can be climbed moving together. The relatively short approach also saves time, time that can be very precious if you are intending to continue on to the Nadelhorn. In fact, as well as being one of the most beautiful traverses in the Valais Alps, this combination also provides the most logical descent. The rock on the jagged ridge is mostly good, but it is rare to have optimal conditions for both parts of the route. When the ridge is dry enough for the rock climbing to be easy, the face is usually hard ice, making the climbing more difficult and much harder on the calf muscles. Conversely, when there are good snow conditions on the face, there is generally enough snow on the ridge to make the traverse more difficult. Most climbers prefer this latter situation.

### APPROACH
Follow the path from the hut to the Hohbalmgletscher, then go up the glacier to the foot of the face.

### NORTH-EAST FACE
Cross the bergschrund and quickly move left until directly below the summit in order to avoid stone fall from the Nadeljoch. Climb straight up to the summit.

### TRAVERSE TO THE NADELHORN
Go down the ridge from the Lenzspitze (4,294m) to the Nadeljoch (4,208m). Continue to the Nadelhorn (4,327m), going over four main gendarmes (good rock, 3, a section of 3c). The slabby descents from these gendarmes can be difficult in icy conditions.

### DESCENT
Continue along the north-east ridge of the Nadelhorn to the Windjoch (3,850m). The difficult sections can be avoided by moving on to the side of the ridge – which side will depend on conditions. Go down the slope below the Windjoch, then traverse across the Hohbalmgletscher (crevasses) to the hut.

*The superb towers on the traverse.*

# VALAIS ALPS

Lenzspitze  Nadelhorn

Allalinhorn, Strahlhorn, Rimpfischhorn and Monte Rosa.

# JEGIGRAT (3,368m)

## SOUTH-EAST SPUR OF THE GRAND GENDARME AND NORTH-EAST–SOUTH-WEST TRAVERSE OF THE JEGIGRAT

**ROAD ACCESS:** A9 motorway to *Sierre-est*, then Visp, Stalden, Saas Grund.
**START POINT:** Weissmies Hut, 2,726m (641'660/110'400). Tel: 027 9572554. 45 mins from the midway station of the Saas Grund–Kreuzboden–Hohsaas gondola lift.
**DIFFICULTY:** South-east Spur of the Grand Gendarme: D, 4c. North-east–South-west Traverse of the Jegigrat: AD, 3c. The foot of the spur is not very easy to make out, as it blends into the surrounding rock.
**TIMES:** approach 2½ hrs; South-east Spur 2½ hrs; traverse of the Jegigrat 2–3 hrs; descent 1½ hrs.
**VERTICAL HEIGHT:** 670m.
**CONDITIONS:** dry rock. Thanks to its sunny aspect and relatively low altitude, the South-east Spur comes into condition quickly after bad weather. A little snow on the traverse of the Jegigrat is not a problem.
**SPECIFIC GEAR:** 40m single rope, six quickdraws. Rock shoes not essential.
**IN SITU GEAR:** bolts on the South-east Spur, *in situ* belays, ring bolts for the abseils from the Jegigrat.
**MAPS:** 1309 Simplon, 1329 Saas.
**FIRST ASCENTS:** South-east Spur: Otmar & Robert Zurbriggen, 6 October 1947.
Jegigrat: Walter Bloch with the guide Theodor Bumann, 14 August 1917.

Lovely climbing on the South-East Spur of the Grand Gendarme.

Hermann Biner's CAS guidebook for the Valais describes several interesting routes on the Jegigrat, above the Weissmies Hut. The South-west–North-east Traverse of the ridge and the South-east Spur of the Grand Gendarme seem to be the most attractive. Michel Vaucher included both these routes in his '100 Best Climbs' book and even suggested linking them – the descent from the traverse of the Jegigrat leads to the foot of the spur, so, if you climb fast enough, you can do the spur and reach the summit of the Grand Gendarme a second time. Then I thought: why not start up the spur and continue along the ridge? However, it isn't easy to ignore the recommendations of such a great mountaineer as Michel Vaucher. Could it be that traversing the ridge from the north-east to the south-west is less worthwhile? The only way to find out was to try it. By the time we had finished our explorations at the Jegihorn gully, we had both drawn the same conclusion – it is a superb combination. Traversing the ridge from the north-east to the south-west did not pose any major problems and some of the climbing was extremely pleasant. As for the spur, it is simply excellent. Put the two together, and the result is one of the best rock climbs in the Saas Valley.

# VALAIS ALPS

## APPROACH
Follow the path north from the hut to the lateral moraine above the Tälli Valley. Go up to the end of the moraine (2,972m), then continue north-eastwards across scree slopes, staying close to the foot of the cliffs. Traverse below the Jegiturm (3,368m), then go up the boulderfield to the foot of the spur.

## SOUTH-EAST SPUR OF THE GRAND GENDARME
Start by climbing the slabs on the left flank of the spur, then move on to the crest and finally the right flank (3, then 4c). Climb the corner to the ridge, then go over the overhang on the right (4). From the foot of an orange wall, head slightly left, then go straight up to a niche (4). Exit rightwards and go up to a 10m black corner. Belay at the foot of the summit wall. Traverse right (horizontal crack, 4) and gain the summit via a wall with abundant holds (4).

## NORTH-EAST–SOUTH-WEST TRAVERSE OF THE JEGIGRAT
Abseil (20m) down the north side of the Grand Gendarme to a ledge. Move back left to regain the ridge at the foot of the gendarme. Follow the ridge, mostly on the crest but occasionally on the south side to avoid the more difficult sections. The climbing on some of the towers is very pleasant but never harder than 3c.

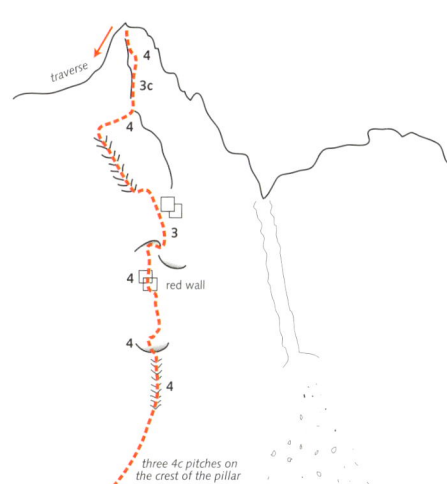

## DESCENT
From spot height 3,350m, go down the scree slope to spot height 3,093m (via ferrata at the end), then descend the easy, south-facing gully (Puiseux Couloir). Follow the path from the foot of the gully back to the hut.

# WEISSMIES (4,023m)

## NORTH RIDGE

**ROAD ACCESS:** see route no.11 (page 38).
**START POINT:** see route no.11 (page 38). A fast team should be able to do the route in a day by taking the first cable car from Saas Grund to Hohsaas.
**DIFFICULTY:** AD+, 4. The crux slab is equipped with a metal bar – best not to fall on to it! Requires a full range of mountaineering skills. The descent can be difficult if there are sections of bare ice. Do not overlook the danger of crevasses.
**TIMES:** approach 2 hrs; climb 4 hrs; descent 2 hrs.
**VERTICAL HEIGHT:** 1,350m.
**CONDITIONS:** dry rock on the North Ridge. Solid snow bridges on the glacier for the descent.
**SPECIFIC GEAR:** 30m rope, crampons, ice axe, four quickdraws, two or three ice screws.
**IN SITU GEAR:** a few pegs and bolts, iron bar at the crux.
**MAPS:** 1309 Simplon, 1329 Saas.
**FIRST ASCENTS:** North Ridge: W.H. Paine, Miss E. Paine with Theodor Andenmatten & P. Zurbriggen, the owner of the Saas Grund hotel, 25 August 1884.
Normal Route: Jakob Christian Häusser with the guide Peter Josef Zurbriggen, late August 1855.

The snowy outline of the Weissmies, the highest peak in a triptych completed by the Fletschhorn and Lagginhorn, is well known to everyone who visits the Saas Valley. Its normal route can be climbed in a day from the lifts at Saas Grund and therefore sees innumerable ascents, even in winter, as it is a top-class ski descent. The name, Weissmies (white foam), could give the impression that this is an entirely snowy peak, but the best route on the mountain, the North Ridge, is essentially a rock climb that follows a narrow thread of schist stretching to the sky. Climbing the North Ridge and descending via the normal route is a superb combination that a fast team should be able to do in a day. Although the rock is not always perfect, the ridge includes some lovely climbing, and the snowy crest leading to the summit is magnificent. Even the descent is superb, with the seracs of the north-west face providing a spectacular finale to one of the greatest mixed climbs on a 4,000m peak in the Valais.

There is still much nice rock climbing to do before you get to the summit dome.

# VALAIS ALPS

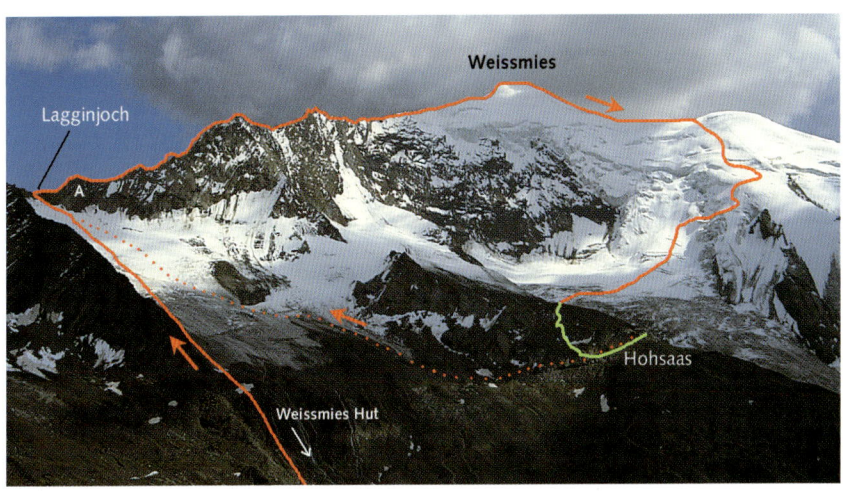

Descent via the normal route.

# WEISSMIES
## NORTH RIDGE

### APPROACH
From the hut, follow the path westwards past spot height 2,892m to the Hohlaubgletscher. Go up the left bank of the glacier to the Lagginjoch (3,499m). At the end of the season, an area of open crevasses may make the standard route up the glacier impassable. In this case, traverse across to the Hohsaas lift station, then head east up the Geissrücken to reach the glacier at around 3,350m.

### NORTH RIDGE
The North Ridge consists of a series of slabs that overhang the east face. Climb the edge of these slabs. Go round a pinnacle by following a ledge of loose rock on the left. A steeper step in the ridge forms the crux – a slab with a peg at its foot and an iron bar in the middle (grade 4). Continue up the crest of the ridge to spot height 3,722m.

Stay on the left to go past an area of poor rock. When the rock improves, go over the summits of all the gendarmes (4) except one, which is turned on the left (slings and abseil rings at its summit). Nice climbing leads to the Ross (horse), which is also traversed along its crest (3c, pegs).

The climbing becomes easier after spot height 3,830m. When the rock ends, follow the snowy ridge (cornices) to the summit.

### DESCENT
The normal route is usually well tracked. Depending on the state of the glacier, route finding through the crevasses can be difficult and care is needed (sections of bare ice and steep ground). The general line follows the north-east side of the shoulder from the dome at 3,815m to just before spot height 3,307m, where it bears diagonally leftwards to avoid an area of crevasses. Traverse above the crevasses (around 3,230m) on the Triftgletscher to its right bank. Follow the edge of the rocks to pick up the path back to Hohsaas (3,101m).

The easy-angled slabs of the north ridge overhang the Laggintal.

# VALAIS ALPS

# BLÜEMLISALPHORN (3,589m) & MORGENHORN (3,668m)

## NORTH FACE AND WEST-EAST TRAVERSE OF THE BLÜEMLISALP RIDGE

**ROAD ACCESS:** from the south, A9 motorway to *Sierre-est*, then Gampel-Steg to Goppenstein and the Lötschberg tunnel. From there, train to Kandersteg. From the north, A1 motorway to Berne, A6 to Spiez, then cantonal road to Kandersteg.
**START POINT:** Blüemlisalp Hut, 2,834m (625'560/151'030). Tel: 033 6761437. 4 hrs from the top of the Kandersteg-Oeschinen chairlift.
**DIFFICULTY:** North Face, D, 45–55°. Traverse, AD, grade-2 rock. Most of the face is easy, the only difficult section being at the top. In good conditions, the traverse is quite straightforward, but bare ice can make the descents on the ridge difficult. Crevasses on the descent from the Morgenhorn.
**TIMES:** approach 1½ hrs; North Face 2–3 hrs; traverse 3–5 hrs; descent 1½ hrs.
**VERTICAL HEIGHT:** 1,080m.
**CONDITIONS:** snow on the face and ridge.
**SPECIFIC GEAR:** 50m rope, six ice screws, six quickdraws, crampons, two ice axes each.
**IN SITU GEAR:** one *in situ* abseil station on the traverse.
**MAP:** 1248 Mürren.
**FIRST ASCENTS:** North Face: Walter Amstutz, Willy Richardet & Hermann Salvisberg, 1 June 1924. Traverse: H. Seymour Hoare with Johann von Bergen, September 1879.

Balancing along the narrow crest of a snowy ridge is one of mountaineering's simplest pleasures. The Alps boasts several classic cornice-fringed ridges, with pride of place being shared by routes such as the Rochefort and Bionnassay ridges in the Mont Blanc range, the Liskamm traverse above Zermatt, and the traverse of Pizzi Palü in the Engadine. The route that interests us here, the traverse of the Blüemlisalp, has many qualities that make it a contender for the number-one spot on this prestigious list. Of course, some of these characteristics, such as the beautiful setting – the Blüemlisalp is encircled by the giants of the Bernese Oberland, short approach and easy descent, are shared by several of its rivals. What sets the Blüemlisalp apart is the possibility of starting the traverse by climbing the mountain's superb north face. The result is a truly memorable outing, combining a short approach from the hut to the foot of the Blüemlisalphorn, a 400m climb on an imposing north face with few objective dangers and a 2km traverse to the Morgenhorn along a splendidly exposed snowy ridge. Your only regret when you get back to the hut will be that the route wasn't longer.

### APPROACH
Follow the path from the hut to the Blüemlisalpgletscher. Go up the eastern branch of the glacier to the saddle to the south of the Ufem Stock. Go over the saddle (around 3,120m) and pick a way past the few crevasses to the foot of the face.

### BLÜEMLISALPHORN: NORTH FACE
The best line will depend on conditions and the presence of objective dangers (few in recent years). The plug of ice below the summit can be turned on the left or on the right.

### WEST-EAST TRAVERSE OF THE BLÜEMLISALP
From the Blüemlisalphorn, go down the narrow snowy ridge. A short abseil is needed to descend a small rock step halfway between the Blüemlisalphorn and the Wyssi Frau. Go up to the summit of the Wyssi Frau. After a short descent on snow, traverse horizontally across to another area of rock, then continue along the ridge to the Morgenhorn.

### DESCENT
There are a few large crevasses to avoid at the top. Descend the north face, either in the middle or on its eastern edge, depending on conditions. Continue down the glacier to join the approach route, which is followed back to the hut.

# BERNESE ALPS

**14**

A heavenly voyage.

# BIETSCHHORN (3,934m)

## EAST SPUR

**ROAD ACCESS:** A9 motorway to *Sierre-est*. Cantonal road to just before Visp, then follow signs to Baltschieder, Ausserberg. Ask at the Hotel Bahnhof (next to the railway station, just before Ausserberg) for permission to continue to spot height 1,264m.

**START POINT:** Baltschiederklause Hut, 2,783m (634'700/138'290). Tel: 027 9522365. 6½ hrs from Ausserberg, 5½ hrs from spot height 1,264m, via Ze Steinu, Martischipfa. The path follows a beautiful irrigation canal. If you have bikes, you can save time by cycling through the tunnel (shown on the map, head torch needed) that starts approx. 200m west of spot height 1,264m, just below the left-hand side of the road (*Stollen* on the signs).

**DIFFICULTY:** D, sections of grade 4, but mostly grade 2 and 3. Long and varied route. Care is needed when descending the north ridge, especially between spot heights 3,706m and 3,477m, and if there is bare ice on the ridge or if you descend very late in the day. If you are intending to descend back to the valley the day you do the route, don't forget that the walk out from the hut is very long.

**TIMES:** approach 2½ hrs; climb 4½–5½ hrs; descent 4 hrs.
**VERTICAL HEIGHT:** 1,170m.
**CONDITIONS:** dry rock on the spur. No ice on the snowy section of the north ridge. Beware of avalanches.
**SPECIFIC GEAR:** 30m rope, four quickdraws, three ice screws, crampons, ice axe.
**IN SITU GEAR:** pegs, a few bolts.
**MAPS:** 1268 Lötschental, 1288 Raron.
**FIRST ASCENT:** C.T. Dent & J. Oakley Maund with J. Jaun & A. Maurer, 25 July 1878.

The Bietschhorn is one of the Alps' great mountains. Clearly visible from the Rhône Valley, its imposing mass is a siren call to mountaineers. Nevertheless, it receives fewer visits than many slightly higher peaks, because the summit does not quite reach the magic altitude of 4000m. But the absence of crowds just adds to the pleasure of climbing its flanks. Despite the long approach from the valley floor and the generally poor quality of the rock, a few of its routes are well worth seeking out. In addition to the once popular south-east ridge, described by Lionel Terray and Louis Lachenal in *Conquistadors of the Useless*, and a few snowy gullies on the east face (Patrick Gabarrou has left his mark), pride of place goes to the East Spur, described here. With an elegant line and good rock, the East Spur is arguably the most aesthetic way of reaching this fabulous summit. When it is combined with a descent via the north ridge, a narrow crest of snow plunging towards the Lötschental, the result is the best moderately difficult route on the mountain. Anyone who remains unconvinced during the climb will surely be won over by the far-reaching views from the summit.

The descent overlooks the Lötschental.

# BERNESE ALPS

## 15

Pleasant climbing leads directly to the summit.

# BIETSCHHORN
## EAST SPUR

### APPROACH
From the hut, head north-west along the path below the cliffs of the Jägihorn to the Üssre Baltschiedergletscher. Circle round leftwards to the foot of the East Spur. To avoid the steep lower section of the spur, cross the bergschrund, often close to the rock, then go up the snow to the start of the route, at a horizontal section of the ridge.

### EAST SPUR
Climb a wide tower (or turn it on the right), then go up the spur, staying as close as possible to the crest. The climbing eases in the upper section and the summit is gained via mixed ground.

### DESCENT
Follow the crest of the ridge to the north summit. From here, either descend the mixed ground on the ridge crest (a few bolts) to spot height 3,706m, or follow a narrow but easy ledge on the western flank of the ridge. Continue down snow to spot height 3,477m, then go down a north-facing rock rib to reach the glacier above the Baltschiederjoch (3,195m). Traverse across the glacier, then follow the path back to the hut.

*Descending the snowy north ridge adds variety to the route.*

# BERNESE ALPS

# STOCKHORN (3,211m)

## SOUTH RIDGE
**ROAD ACCESS:** see route no.15 (page 48).
**START POINT:** Stockhorn Bivouac, 2,598m (634'040/136'320). Booking not possible. Gas cooker, pans and blankets provided. (To light the cooking stove, keep the knob pushed in for several seconds after lighting the gas.)
**ACCESS:** PD, 5 hrs from spot height 1,264m. A lovely walk beside a canal that has been in use since 1371. Getting to the bivouac involves climbing chains and ladders. Can be slippery in wet weather. Water can be obtained by melting snow from the cirque above the hut. Later in the season, this snow may have all melted, so water bottles should be filled from streams before getting to the hut.
**DIFFICULTY:** TD, 5c oblig. (5a oblig. if you follow the historic route from the top of the fifth tower.) Given the length of the route and the lack of easy escape routes, the climb should only be attempted in stable weather. The rock is good on the difficult sections but requires care elsewhere. Only for experienced mountaineers who will find this long route superb.
**TIMES:** approach 15 mins; climb 6–8 hrs; descent 1½ hrs.
**VERTICAL HEIGHT:** 650m
**CONDITIONS:** dry rock. Rapidly in condition after bad weather.
**SPECIFIC GEAR:** 50m single rope (55m is ideal for the abseil from the fourth tower), 10 quickdraws, rock shoes for the fifth tower, small and medium cams.
**IN SITU GEAR:** numerous bolts and pegs in the difficult sections. The *in situ* gear is well placed and takes nothing away from the pleasure of the climbing.
**MAPS:** 1268 Lötschental, 1288 Raron.
**FIRST ASCENT:** R. Aubert, A. Collini, R. Dittert, R. Lambert, F. Marullaz, G. de Rham, C. Thévenaz, A. Tissières & J. Weigle, 17 June 1945.

Of all the rock climbs described in these pages, the South Ridge of the Stockhorn is probably the most demanding. First, there is its technical difficulty. The crux pitch, on the fifth tower, is superb, but it involves 'solid' 5+ climbing, done carrying a heavy sack. Second, the route is very long, involving 650m of climbing from the start to the summit. Finally, the starting point, a CAS bivouac, is one of the least accessible huts in the Alps. But, as we all know, in the mountains, everything is relative. So, when you get to the hut, think back to before it was built, when mountaineers heading for the Stockhorn had to bivouac under the stars at Martischipfa, almost 650m lower than the current shelter. While climbing the chains in the access gully in broad daylight, spare a thought for those who passed this way before 1971, when the hut was built. Similarly, when you get to the summit of the Stockhorn and see the interminable ridge stretching away to the Bietschhorn, let your understandable pride at completing this difficult climb be tempered by the accounts of your predecessors in the hut book (Stockhorn Südgrat-Bietschhorn). Some, who did not want what is one of the best rock climbs in the Bernese Alps to end, continued along the arête to a second bivouac and then climbed the south-east ridge of the Bietschhorn, another grade-5 climb but with much less fixed gear. Still, my companion and I were quite proud and very pleased with ourselves to have done just the fabulous South Ridge of the Stockhorn.

### SOUTH RIDGE
Go up the grassy terraces above the hut to the ridge. After a short distance, move right (cairns). Follow the crest to a notch, followed by a grade-4 wall. Move slightly right (peg) after the second bolt. Descend the north side of the first tower for a few metres, then do a 10m abseil. Continue easily along a ledge on the left, then move back on to the ridge crest at the foot of the second tower.

# BERNESE ALPS

Traverse left slightly, then move back on to the ridge and follow it to the foot of a wall (bolt). Climb a crack (4, bolt and peg) that widens into a chimney. Belay at the top of the chimney. Traverse left slightly and climb a gully. Move back right to a small notch on the ridge crest, which is followed to the top of the second tower. Abseil (10m) into the notch at the foot of the third tower. Climb this tower (3-4), then climb down into the following notch (3, stepped ledges with lots of holds). Go up to the foot of the summit wall of the fourth tower. Avoid this wall by going along an exposed ledge to an abseil station. Abseil down to the foot of the fifth tower (one or two abseils depending on whether you have a 55m rope or a 50m rope). Bolts and pegs show the line of the direct route up the fifth tower (see topo).

P1: 35m, 5, two-bolt belay.

P2: 20m, 3, block belay.

P3: 20m, 5, two-bolt belay (the least comfortable on the fifth tower).

P4: 30m, 5c (one move at the beginning and for the exit chimney), bolt belay.

The historic variant (less *in situ* gear) traverses 5m left in the middle of pitch 2, at a red and black mark on the rock (bolt in the black rock), and then goes up a short wall (one peg) before traversing left (bolts) to a good crack. Move left from the crack to belay on a large ledge (belay hidden, don't climb too high, 4/4c). Move back on to the ridge (slightly higher than the top of the direct variant, 3-4). Follow the crest of the ridge to the top of the fifth tower, turning any difficulties on the left (4). Nice climbing along the crest leads to the highest point (3, 4, two steps before the summit).

## DESCENT

Descend parallel to the east ridge, following easy, scree-covered ledges on its north side to an obvious notch. Move on to the south side and continue down the ridge, sometimes on the crest, sometimes just below the crest. Just after spot height 3,014m (the ridge turns east again), descend a gully on the left. Trend rightwards across an area of easy scree to a saddle (cairn) looking across to the Rote Wand (impressive red wall).

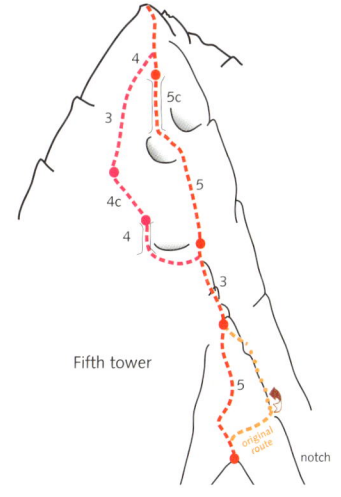

Abseil from an *in situ* belay 10m south of the saddle. Walk down to the next abseil point, bearing right (cairn, abseil slings can be seen at the saddle). Follow a faint path along the foot of the Rote Wand, then move back left across the gully that leads down to the scree slopes. Go down the scree to the bivouac.

# MÖNCH (4,107m)

## NOLLEN

**ROAD ACCESS:** from the north, A1 motorway to Berne, A6 to *Interlaken-Ost*, then cantonal road to Grindelwald. From the south, A9 motorway to *Sierre-est*, then cantonal road to Gampel-Steg and the Lötschberg Tunnel. Put your car on the train (CHF 27 one way during the week, CHF 29.50 at weekends) to Kandersteg. Then Spiez, A6 motorway to *Interlaken-Ost*, then Grindelwald.

**START POINT:** Guggi Hut, 2,791m (641'080/156'970). Tel: 033 8553157. Staffed intermittently from late June to mid-September. 3 hrs from the Eigergletscher station on the Grindelwald–Jungfraujoch railway. Waymarked mountain path.
For the return, the entrance to the train tunnels is to the east of the Sphinx observatory, close to spot height 3,464m.

**DIFFICULTY:** D, one pitch at 55–60°. The difficulties are concentrated in an area of ice called the Nollen. Risk of wind slabs after fresh snowfalls.

**TIMES:** climb 6–8 hrs; descent 1½–2 hrs.

**VERTICAL HEIGHT:** 1,330m.

**CONDITIONS:** little or no snow on the approach. The Nollen is usually hard ice. Good freezing conditions at night are essential.

**SPECIFIC GEAR:** 50m rope, four quickdraws, six to eight ice screws for the party, crampons, two ice axes each.

**MAP:** 1249 Finsteraarhorn.

**FIRST ASCENT:** Edmund von Fellenberg with Christian Michel & Peter Egger, 13 July 1866.

The Eiger-Mönch-Jungfrau triptych mesmerises the tourists who come up to Kleine Scheidegg in the train from Grindelwald. Despite being sandwiched between the monumental north face of the Eiger and the equally massive north face of the Jungfrau, the Mönch is no shrinking violet and every climber's eye is immediately drawn to the Nollen, the huge swathe of ice on the west side of the face. Nollen is also the name of a classic route that exploits what is probably the only true weakness in the trio's northern defences. But classic doesn't mean easy, and you will be happy you sharpened your axes when you are doing battle with the crux pitch. Modern techniques have taken a lot of the sting out of climbing steep glaciers, but scaling 50m of hard ice at an angle of 60° or more is still quite a challenge. The rest of the route will feel easy once you have dispatched this pitch! At the summit, the atmosphere changes completely, as the steep and forbidding walls of the north face give way to the open icy expanses of the Aletsch basin.

In the shadow of the Eiger.

# BERNESE ALPS

17

The Guggiroute seen from the hut – a true eagle's nest.

# MÖNCH
## NOLLEN

What is more, the south face provides an easy normal route that quickly takes you back to civilisation. It is so nice to be whisked down to Grindelwald in a nice, comfortable train ...

### NOLLEN

Go up the scree-covered slabs above the hut to the wall above the Mönchplateau (start of the path shown on the 1:25,000-scale map). It is usual to stay to the left of the wall when going up. A few cairns indicate the zigzag route to the Mönchplateau (3,112m). Continue up rocks and snow, first heading east, then south-east. The slope becomes steeper as it approaches the

Eiger, Mönch, Jungfrau – a formidable bastion.

# BERNESE ALPS

tongue of the Nollen, which provides the crux pitch. In most years the angle is between 55 and 60°, but it can be slightly greater. At the end of the difficulties, cross a plateau, then go up towards the ridge on the edge of the north-west face. The best line (rock or snow) will depend on conditions. Once on the crest, go up to the south-west ridge, which is followed to the summit.

### DESCENT
Go down the snowy crest of the east ridge. Bear right, then climb down an area of mixed ground (*in situ* runners) to spot height 3,887m. Head due south down easy rocks to the snow. Follow the well-trodden track to the Jungfraujoch station.

# SCHRECKHORN (4,078m)

## SOUTH PILLAR

**ROAD ACCESS:** see route no.17 (page 54).
**START POINT:** Schreckhorn Hut, 2,529m (650'600/159'150). Tel: 033 855 10 25. 4½ hrs from the top of the Grindelwald-Pfingstegg gondola lift, via Stieregg and Rots Gufer.
**DIFFICULTY:** TD, 5. A long and magnificent route at altitude. Sustained climbing in the upper section.
**TIMES:** approach 3–3½ hrs; climb 5–6 hrs; descent 4–5 hrs. It takes about 3 hrs to get from the hut back to the lift, so it is worth spending two nights in the hut – if you miss the last lift, it is a 3,000m descent from the summit to Grindelwald!
**VERTICAL HEIGHT:** 1,600m.
**CONDITIONS:** dry rock, quickly comes into condition after bad weather.
**SPECIFIC GEAR:** 50m single rope, crampons, ice axe, rock shoes, set of nuts and small to large cams, six to eight quickdraws.
**IN SITU GEAR:** a few pegs, *in situ* abseil stations for the descent.
**MAP:** 1229 Grindelwald.
**FIRST ASCENT:** H. Kocher, P. Luzuy, R. Perrenoud & P. Girardin, 24 July 1955.

Schreckhorn, the 'horn of fear'; with such a name it is difficult to imagine this 4,000m peak in the Oberland could have many attractions. This would certainly have been the case in the past, as the peasants of days gone by would have viewed the seemingly impregnable fortress of the Schreckhorn with fear and revulsion.

The rock is perfect all the way.

But when mountaineers began looking at the heights as more than just places to survive, its flanks were found to be a fabulous playground. Even the normal route provides one of the most enjoyable easy climbs on a 4,000m peak in the Alps. On the other side of the mountain, the north-west ridge (Andersongrat) has magnificent views, while the traverse from the Schreckhorn to the Lauteraarhorn is also a great classic that allows peak baggers to tick two 4,000m summits in one long and demanding route. However, the Schreckhorn's brightest jewel is the South Pillar. Lost in the immensity of the mountain's south face, the pillar is very discreet, much less striking than the Bonatti Pillar on the Drus, for example, but you quickly appreciate the elegant line and superb granite as soon as you start climbing this graceful column. The ochre-coloured rock contrasting against the white expanses of the area's glaciers inspires contemplation. However, the sparseness of the *in situ* gear and the need to climb grade-5 pitches with heavy sacks mean the South Pillar should not be underestimated. This is a serious undertaking and one of the best routes at this level of difficulty on a 4,000m peak.

# BERNESE ALPS

The promise of a great route ...

# SCHRECKHORN
## SOUTH PILLAR

### APPROACH
From the hut, go down to the tongue of the Obers Ischmeer. Continue south along the right bank of the glacier to go past the two tongues of the Schreckfirn. Go across a rib of rock (paint marks on the polished slabs beside the glacier just before the rib), then head east up a debris slope. Follow a faint path to the saddle of Gaag (rocks at the end), then head north-east across and up a steep snow slope (care needed if bare ice). Cross the Schreckfirn to get to the bergschrund, which is crossed slightly to the left of the gully on the south face (up to here, this is the same as the normal route).

### SOUTH PILLAR
Climb easy rocks on the right bank of a snowy gully. Move right under an overhang at the foot of the pillar to gain a snow or ice gully. Go up the gully to a slabby rib, which is climbed in two pitches. When it becomes vertical, traverse right (ledge) to a parallel rib. Climb this rib to below an overhang,

Walking up to the Schreckhorn Hut.

The Finsteraarhorn, on the left, reigns over the glacial expanse of the Obers Ischmeer.

# BERNESE ALPS

then exit left. Continue up a gully for one pitch (grade 3 and 4 up to here, pegs) and reach a large ledge at the foot of a wall. Traverse 20m left, then climb straight up towards a vertical corner-crack. Follow it for 30m to get to a niche below a roof (5, crux, four pegs). Climb a smooth, vertical wall on the right (5, one peg) and move on to the ridge on the right. Climb a slab with thin cracks (5, two pegs). Climb two direct pitches (3), then go along a horizontal ledge to avoid a smooth arête.

A vertical chimney (5) leads back on to the ridge. Climb the last step directly (4). Descend into a notch, then gain the south-west summit. Easy rocks lead to the true summit.

## DESCENT

Go down the south-west ridge, the upper step of which is equipped for abseiling. From the shoulder on the south-west ridge, head left down stepped ledges to the Schreckfirn and the foot of the pillar.

# KLEIN SIMELISTOCK (2,384m)
# & GROSS SIMELISTOCK (2,482m)

## NORTH-SOUTH TRAVERSE

**ROAD ACCESS:** A1 motorway to Berne, A6 to Interlaken, cantonal road to Meiringen, then mountain road to Rosenlaui.
**START POINT:** Engelhörn Hut, 1,901m (656'170/170'480). Tel: 033 9714726.
1½ hrs from Rosenlaui.
**DIFFICULTY:** AD+, 4b. Rock sometimes poor on the Klein Simelistock. Sometimes exposed but well-protected climbing on the Gross Simelistock. Complex route finding on the descent.
**TIMES:** approach 1 hr; Klein Simelistock 1½ hrs; Gross Simelistock 1½ hrs; descent 1½ hrs.
**VERTICAL HEIGHT:** 650m.
**CONDITIONS:** dry rock. The descent can be tricky in wet conditions.
**SPECIFIC GEAR:** 50m rope, eight quickdraws, small and medium cams.
**IN SITU GEAR:** a few pegs and bolts, ring bolts for the abseils.
**MAPS:** 1210 Innertkirchen, 1229 Grindelwald, 1230 Guttanen.
**FIRST ASCENT:** Hans Brog & Oskar Neiger with Niklaus Kohler, 16 August 1913.

Which part of the route leaves the greatest impression? For many it will be the first time they enter the Ochsental, back on terra firma at the end of the descent from the Simelisattel. Hemmed in by huge precipices, it feels like a different world. But many other factors contribute to making this outing unforgettable. Once the climbing is over, you will have the time to look back upon the exposed moves that led my friend to say, 'it's a good job we brought the rope', upon the wonderful climbing on the summit ridge of the Gross Simelistock, upon the complexities and uncertainties of the descent – chamois country par excellence, and upon the spectacular backdrop of huge cliffs set against the verdant pastures of the Oberland.

One thing is certain, you will be eager to return and once again revel in the unique atmosphere of the Engelhörner basin.

### APPROACH

From the hut, follow the path along the right bank of the Ochsental. At around 2,000m, bear north along a fainter path that ends near a gully. Go up steeply on the right to where the path starts again. Go up grassy slopes to a saddle at the foot of the rock ridge.

# BERNESE ALPS

# KLEIN & GROSS SIMELISTOCK
## NORTH–SOUTH TRAVERSE

The descent route.

## KLEIN SIMELISTOCK: NORTH-WEST RIDGE

Start directly above the saddle via a small gully (3b). Continue in the same direction until you can see a cairn on the ridge to the right. Move on to the crest of the ridge (2) and follow it all the way to the summit (3b). The line is obvious, but here are a few details. Climb a sharp section of the ridge on its left edge (one bolt, belay after 25m, behind the crest). Descend slightly to a notch. The summit step, preceded by slabs, is quite wide. Climb the easiest line.

## GROSS SIMELISTOCK: TRAVERSE FROM THE KLEIN SIMELISTOCK SOUTH-WEST RIDGE

Do a 20m abseil to get to the notch between the two summits. Follow the joining ridge to the foot of the summit cone of the Gross Simelistock. Go right round a large protruding block (3b) by climbing on to a narrow ledge with barely enough room for the feet (ring bolt, exposed) and then going straight up. Belay on the block, beside a slot. Traverse along a wide, easy ledge on the west face to the foot of the south-west ridge. Go straight up for 10m (4b, crux, good holds but a little polished). Belay on the crest. Head diagonally rightwards to a deep chimney. Climb the chimney (4b, awkward exit). It is also possible to go straight up from the belay at the same grade. Finish up the lovely summit ridge (3b).

### DESCENT

The first abseil ring can be seen 30m below the summit, on the ridge to the south. This is reached by briefly following the north-east ridge and then a grassy crack. Do three 15m abseils to get to the Simelisattel (2,426m).

From the saddle, go down the rocky combe on the right to a step. Do a short abseil, followed by another abseil. Gain a grassy shoulder, then head left (cairn) to a steep gully. Go down this gully (abseil possible but easy to walk down). Climb down the final terrace, next to a small pinnacle on the left, staying on the left. This leads to a vast area of slabs. Descend for about 50m, staying on the right, then traverse diagonally leftwards to the southern edge of the slabs (do not traverse too low, as there is a huge hole further down). Continue down grassy slopes to easy slabs. Further down, a rock tooth can be seen next to a small saddle (cairn). Go down to the rock tooth, then descend rightwards to a belay. Abseil (20m) down the gully, then go down easy scree slopes to the Ochsental.

# BERNESE ALPS

Just before the summit of the Klein Simelistock.

# GROSS DIAMANTSTOCK (3,162m)

## EAST RIDGE

**ROAD ACCESS:** A1 motorway to Berne, A6 to Interlaken, Meiringen, then cantonal road to Guttannen, Handegg, Räterichsbodensee dam.
**START POINT:** Bächlital Hut, 2,328m (664'680/159'870). Tel: 033 9731114. 2 hrs from the dam.
**DIFFICULTY:** D, 4c. Several pitches of grade-4 climbing. Escape possible to the south in a few places.
**TIMES:** approach 1½ hrs; climb 3½–4½ hrs; descent 2½–3 hrs. Be careful when descending the snowfield if it is late in the day (risk of snow slides).
**VERTICAL HEIGHT:** 850m.
**CONDITIONS:** dry rock. The moderate altitude means the route quickly comes into condition after bad weather.
**SPECIFIC GEAR:** 50m single rope, small and medium cams, six quickdraws, crampons. An ice axe is not always necessary, as the snowfield on the east face is not very steep and the traverse can be protected. Rock shoes not essential.
**IN SITU GEAR:** bolts and pegs.
**MAP:** 1230 Guttannen.
**FIRST ASCENT:** Hans Baer & companions, 4 July 1937.

What makes the ideal rock route? The answer to this question is, of course, highly subjective, but all climbers would probably agree on a few points. Hence, the perfect climb will be long but not excessively so, have good rock, nice moves, a logical line, escape options if the weather turns and enough *in situ* gear to keep the boldness of the climbing and the weight of your harness within reasonable limits without removing all excitement. In addition, it will have an approach that is not disproportionately long, good and varied views, a high-mountain atmosphere, a well-known summit with a view worthy of the name and no major objective dangers. Every experienced alpinist can name several routes that meet these criteria, and those who have been lucky enough to climb the Gross Diamantstock are likely to include the East Ridge on their list. Of course, good-quality climbs are usually very popular, which can have its disadvantages, but there is little danger of stone fall on the East Ridge and there are many places where slower teams can be overtaken. So, if you are blessed with good weather and your ascent is not marred by unforeseen circumstances, you are sure to finish the day with a big grin on your face. A grin that will be reflected in the Bächlital Hut warden's charming smile – another great reason to come back.

The first pitch of a dream route.

### APPROACH

From the hut, head west along the waymarked trail to the glacier. Go up the glacier tongue, bearing right around an area of crevasses. At around 2,600m, head right off the glacier and go up a snow and scree slope (tracks) to gain the foot of the ridge at Undri Bächli-Licken (2,746m).

# BERNESE ALPS

**20**

Gross Diamantstock

Undri Bächli-Licken

## EAST RIDGE
Climb the first step, staying a few metres to the left of the ridge crest (4c, 4b). Just before the top, move on to the south face and descend to a notch. Follow the crest to a short abseil. Move back on to the ridge via a short, wide crack on the south side (4b). Descend 2m to the foot of the next step. Go up to a thin, horizontal crack and follow it to a corner. Climb the corner and stepped ledges to get back on to the ridge (4a). Easier ground leads to the foot of the next step. Escape possible down the snow to the left. Climb diagonally across the south side of the next step, then go straight up a corner-crack (4a). Go over the next gendarme, staying high on its south face, then descend 10m to a notch.

Continue to the next notch (exposed traverse, bolt) at the foot of a distinctive step. Escape possible on the south face (two 20m abseils). Stay on the left of the ridge crest and cross the slabby step (4c).

Continue straight up above the belay (two pegs), then head right along a chimney-crack (4b). Continue along the crest (the line to the left is much less enjoyable) to the summit, which is gained by climbing either a steep crack on the left (3c) or easy blocks on the north face.

## DESCENT
Follow the easy south-west ridge to the cairn that marks the junction with the east face, just past the southern edge of the snowfield on the east face. Traverse north-east across the snowfield. An obvious diagonal path (cairns) leads to the first abseil rings, which are not needed if there is no snow. A third, bombproof belay can be reached easily by continuing down for 10m below the second abseil ring. Abseil possible just before the bergschrund (belay sometimes hidden under snow). Follow the approach path back to the hut.

# GROSS BIELENHORN (3,210m)

## SOUTH-EAST RIDGE

**ROAD ACCESS:** from the Valais, A9 motorway to *Sierre-est*, then cantonal road to Brig, Furkapass. From Berne, A1 motorway to Berne, A6 to Interlaken, then cantonal road to Meiringen, Grimselpass, Gletsch, Furkapass. From Tessin, A2 motorway to Airolo, Gotthard Tunnel (frequent traffic jams), then cantonal road to Andermatt, Furkapass.
**START POINT:** Sidelen Hut, 2,708m (675'720/161'160). Tel: 041 8870233. 1 hr from spot height 2,280m (car park) on the Uri side of the Furkapass.
**DIFFICULTY:** D, 5+. Several pitches of grade-4 climbing, two grade-5 moves, not obligatory. A sure foot and good route finding abilities are needed for the descent.
**TIMES:** approach 45 mins; climb 4 hrs; descent 2½ hrs.
**VERTICAL HEIGHT:** 520m.
**CONDITIONS:** dry rock. The season is quite long, starting as soon as the Furkapass is open (usually early June). Possible snowfields on the approach and descent.
**SPECIFIC GEAR:** 50m single rope, rock shoes, six quickdraws. Nuts and cams not needed.
**IN SITU GEAR:** bolts.
**MAP:** 1231 Urseren.
**FIRST ASCENT:** A. & O. Amstad, G. Masetto, 19 August 1935.

The South-east Ridge of the Gross Bielenhorn may be very close to the east-south-east ridge of the Gross Furkahorn, but the two routes have totally different characters. The climbing on the Gross Bielenhorn is steep, with superb runnels and rounded holds, whereas the Gross Furkahorn is very slabby, and the sharpness of the crest demands a very different climbing style. Together, these two routes nicely epitomise the area's extraordinary potential.

The granite here is a delight to climb on. The Gross Furkahorn is on the left, with the Gross Bielenhorn on the right in the background.

# CENTRAL SWITZERLAND

## 21

The top section of the South-east Ridge route (main diagram, left) is on the south-west face (inset, above).

# GROSS BIELENHORN
## SOUTH-EAST RIDGE

The first pitch.

### APPROACH
From the hut, head north-east up the path towards the distinctive towers of the Kamel. Go up the left-hand scree-filled gully to the saddle (Untere Bielenlücke) at the foot of the South-east Ridge.

The lower section of the ridge is not very interesting and can be avoided on the right (one or two sections of grade-2 climbing, scree, a few cairns) to reach the first step, above a grassy terrace.

### SOUTH-EAST RIDGE
**P1:** Open corner to the right of the crest. 4a.
**P2:** Easy, a few blocks. 3a.
**P3:** Nice, rounded runnels. 5c (or 4c with two p.a.)
**P4:** Short descent, then go up the right side of the crest. 4.

The granite is wonderfully rough all the way to the summit.

# CENTRAL SWITZERLAND

P5: Straight up a sort of chimney. 4c.
P6: Move right to go round a tower, short descent before the belay. 4c.
P7: Walk along a horizontal ledge to a notch. Belay in the notch.
P8: Straight above the notch, then left. 5c (or one p.a.)
P9: Straight up at first, then right before a corner. 4a.
P10: Go right round the red, rocky pinnacle and then follow the ridge to an abseil. 4a.

Do a 10m abseil on the west face, then traverse to the foot of the summit block.

The east summit is reached either by following the ridge on the right (a few strenuous but easy moves), or by staying on the face to the left (2–3).

## DESCENT

Do a 20m abseil down the west face of the east summit. Easily climb down rock- and mud-filled gullies and ledges to the narrow notch to the north of the red tower. From the notch, do a 25m abseil down the east face. Continue rightwards (scuff marks on the rock) to a line of three 20m abseils (chains, the first abseil station is just below on the left as you descend), which lead to easy ground on the east face. Head back to the saddle near the Kamel and the hut.

*The middle section of the route does not always follow the ridge.*

# SCHIJENSTOCK (3,161M)

## SOUTH RIDGE

**ROAD ACCESS:** from the north, A2 motorway to Lucerne, then cantonal road to Altdorf, Göschenen, minor road up the Göschener Tal. From the Valais, A9 motorway to *Sierre-est*, then cantonal road to Brig, Furkapass, Andermatt, Göschenen, then as above. From the south, A2 motorway to Airolo, Göschenen, then as above.
**START POINT:** Bergsee Hut, 2,370m (680'080/167'890). Tel: 041 8851435. 1½ hrs from the Göscheneralpsee dam.
**DIFFICULTY:** AD, 4a. Numerous abseils. Large sections have to be climbed moving together in order to save time.
**TIMES:** approach 1 hr; climb 5-6 hrs; descent 1 hr.
**VERTICAL HEIGHT:** 790m.
**CONDITIONS:** best when the north-east face is snow free, so you don't have to carry crampons and ice axe for the descent.
**SPECIFIC GEAR:** 50m rope, nuts 5-8, medium cams, six quickdraws.
**IN SITU GEAR:** a few bolts and pegs, cables and rings for the abseils.
**MAP:** 1231 Urseren.
**FIRST ASCENT:** O. Gerecht, A.-E. Meier & F. Wörndle, 1948.

The summit appears deceptively close.

Say you have done the Schijenstock and any climber who knows the mountain is likely to ask: 'Did you do the ridge with nine towers?' Some of the towers on this granite spur go by almost unnoticed, but the route never seems to be able to decide whether it wants to go up or down, and those who are not too keen on abseiling will eventually start thinking 'not another one'. In fact, there are only five abseils, which is not an excessive number, if your rope work is efficient. More importantly, there are also several pitches of wonderful climbing and you are unlikely to be bothered by crowds – the Schijenstock attracts far fewer people than the neighbouring Bergseeschijen, whose south ridge is ascended by a never-ending stream of climbers every fine weather day. The Bergseeschijen owes its classic status to its shorter approach, the more reasonable length of the climbing and the fact that it doesn't involve abseils, but it doesn't quite have enough character to make it a great alpine route. This cannot be said of the Schijenstock, whose rugged charm is enhanced by the extensive views, which stretch all the way from the glacier fields of the Dammastock to the high mountains of the Valais and the Sustenhorn to the north-west.

# CENTRAL SWITZERLAND

**22**

## APPROACH
From the hut, follow the path to the south ridge of the Bergseeschijen for a short distance. In order to avoid knocking stones down, it is possible to go across the grassy slopes above the slabs that can be seen to the north. Go up the vast scree slope that leads to the saddle where the climb starts (a few cairns, faint path). Beware of stone fall in the gully leading to the saddle.

## SOUTH RIDGE
The first part of the ridge is easy and can be climbed moving together. Slightly steeper ground (3a) then leads to an exposed, horizontal section just before the foot of the first step. Follow a crack on the right (one peg, then easy to protect with cams, 4a). Traverse left before the top of the tower (peg visible). Abseil (25m) into the following notch (two pegs in the notch). Easy climbing (grade 3, abandoned Friend) leads to another notch (belay on two pegs, 2m apart and at the same height). For the following step, go up a short wall and exit on to the slab on the right. Continue to the top of the tower (two pegs, 3 and 4a). There is a small notch before the next tower, which is climbed easily (3a). Abseil (25m) into the notch before the next tower. Climb to the top of this tower (one peg, grade 3), then abseil (25m) to the foot of another step, staying on the west side. This step can be climbed moving together (grade 2). 25m abseil.

Go across easy ground (grade 2, go round the west side of the top of the next step) to the foot of a more difficult section. Climb to the second bolt, then traverse right to a peg. The crack that follows is easy to protect with nuts (4, you can also follow the line of bolts, but the climbing is harder).

Higher up, regain the line of bolts and belay on a blocky terrace. Traverse left, then go straight up (4a, go round the west side of the top of the step). Start the final tower on the right (gully, 3a), then head left along a ramp-crack to the crest (3, peg on the crest). Continue up the crest to the top of the tower (4a). Abseil (25m) into the notch below the summit. The easier (2, then 3a) upper section of the ridge is climbed mostly on the right of the crest.

## DESCENT
Follow the east ridge, at first staying around 20m below the crest on the north side. Move left above the glacier overlooking the Schijenstock to the north (a few cairns). Towards the bottom, move back right to directly below the first notch on the east ridge (cairns), noted during the approach. Abseil to the notch, then do a second abseil to reach the gully to the south. Go down this gully to the foot of the cliffs (stone fall possible if several teams in the gully). Go down scree and grassy slopes to the hut.

# SALBITSCHIJEN (2,981m)

## SOUTH RIDGE

**ROAD ACCESS:** see route no.22 (page 72).
**START POINT:** Salbit Hut, 2,105m (685'180/170'080). Tel: 041 8851431. 2½ hrs from Ulmi, spot height 1,195m on the Göschener Tal road, via Regliberg. For a small sum, you can have your sacks taken up to the small chalet halfway up to the hut, but you will have to make the request in German. Cable-lift and telephone 100m east of the car park.
**DIFFICULTY:** TD, 5a obligatory (5c+, one p.a.). Sustained climbing. Some bold moves above protection (both fixed and natural).
**TIMES:** approach 1–1½ hrs; climb 5–7 hrs; descent 1–1½ hrs.
**VERTICAL HEIGHT:** 875m.
**CONDITIONS:** best done when the north-east face is snow free, so you don't have to carry crampons and ice axe for the descent. In this case, approach shoes are sufficient.
**SPECIFIC GEAR:** 50m rope (possible to abseil off the ridge in several places if you use double 50m ropes), small (two sets) and medium cams, eight quickdraws, rock shoes.
**IN SITU GEAR:** bolts and a few pegs.
**MAPS:** 1211 Meiental, 1231 Urseren.
**FIRST ASCENT:** A. & O. Amstad, G. Masetto, 1935.

Looking across from the South Ridge to the jagged West Ridge, with the Dammastock rising in the background.

According to the Salbit guidebook this is 'the best granite ridge in the Alps'. Such claims can only ever be subjective but no one would argue against including Salbitschijen's South Ridge in any book dedicated to the best mountain routes in Switzerland. It has everything the rock climber looks for: perfect rock (it's hard to imagine better), a relatively short approach to a long climb, an aesthetic line, bolts where needed without being over protected, few abseils, an easy-to-follow descent and no complex rope work. Pitch after pitch, all the way to the summit, you will find yourself thinking: 'That has to be the best pitch, there can't be anything better higher up'. When hanging from the belays, your gaze will inevitably be drawn to the neighbouring West Ridge. Absorbed by the difficulties of the South Ridge, you hardly dare imagine what Salbit's other legendary ridge must be like. With its 32 pitches of up to 6b climbing (5c+ obligatory) and vertiginous abseils, the route is so long, many teams end up bivouacking. Whether you are tempted by such a long and difficult climb, or whether you prefer more reasonable objectives, the abundance of great climbs around the Salbit Hut make a return visit to this granite paradise difficult to resist.

# CENTRAL SWITZERLAND

**23**

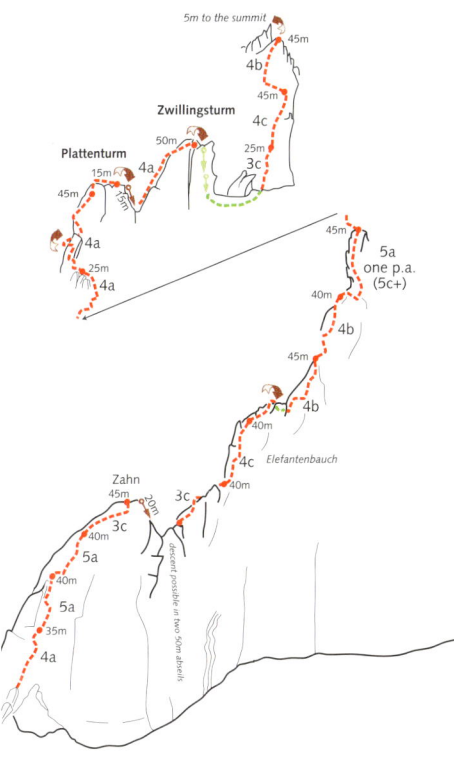

# SALBITSCHIJEN
## SOUTH RIDGE

### APPROACH
From the hut, follow the path west towards the grassy gully that leads to the South Ridge. Go up the gully (chains, beware of stone fall if there are other teams in the gully). From the saddle, head right along the path, going down for a few metres. Go up the rock and grass slope (one or two narrow sections) to a large ledge. Go past a short wall on the right, then head down to the first belay.

Abseil on the South Ridge.

### SOUTH RIDGE
**P1:** 4a.
**P2:** Exit left at the *in situ* sling. 5a.
**P3:** 5a.
**P4:** Look for the bolts on the left, on the traverse at the start. From the belay, continue along the ridge to the abseil station at its end. Abseil into the notch, then go up easily to the next belay. 3c.
**P5** and **P6:** 3c, 4c.
**P7:** Turn one or two towers on the left. Do not be tempted into the wide crack that goes off right. Bolt visible 1m below the crest on the right. 4b.
**P8:** After about 30m you get to a bombproof belay (bolt and maillon, top of a route on the east face). Ignore this belay and continue 10m higher, climbing just to the left of the crest (nut protection) to the belay on the South Ridge. 4b.
**P9:** Crux, 5c+ (5a, one p.a.).
**P10:** 4a.
**P11:** Go left round the top of the needle (sling round a spike). Move back right at the end. 4a.
**P12:** The ridge is narrow and exposed for a few metres after the belay. Climb just to the left of the crest (well protected – sling on a spike and cam in the crack). 4a.
**Transition to P13:** Abseil to a notch, then do another abseil on the left to get to the path that goes round the next tower. The climbing begins again in the notch on the north side of this tower.
**P13:** 3c.
**P14** and **P15:** Two superb pitches provide a magnificent finale: 4c, 4b.

**Exit on to the summit:** Move on to the north side of the ridge and follow the red marks leftwards to the summit needle, which is climbed on its eastern edge (4b). Descend by a 15m abseil on the north face.

### DESCENT
It is a good idea to stay roped up.
Follow the red paint marks (a few cables and cairns), starting down the north-east face, and then going down the right bank of the gully that channels the runoff from the Salbitgletscher (path). Cross the stream and follow the path back to the hut.

# CENTRAL SWITZERLAND

23

# PONCIONE DI CASSINA BAGGIO (2,860m)

## SOUTH RIDGE

**ROAD ACCESS:** from the Valais, A9 motorway to *Sierre-est*, then cantonal road to Brig, Ulrichen, Nufenenpass, All'Acqua. From the south, A2 motorway to Airolo, then cantonal road to Val Bedretto, All'Acqua.
**START POINT:** Piansecco Hut, 1,982m (679'280/149'760). Tel: 091 8691214. 1 hr from All'Acqua.
**DIFFICULTY:** AD, 3, not very sustained. Best climbed moving together in order to save time.
**TIMES:** approach 1¼ hrs; climb 4 hrs; descent 1½–2 hrs.
**VERTICAL HEIGHT:** 920m.
**CONDITIONS:** dry rock, although a little snow should not pose any problems.
**SPECIFIC GEAR:** 50m rope, four quickdraws.
**IN SITU GEAR:** a few pegs.
**MAP:** 1251 Val Bedretto.
**FIRST ASCENTS:** the first ascent of the entire South Ridge is unknown. The upper section, from the notch between the second and third towers, was first climbed by Gabriel de Choudens, Marcel Kurz & Robert Mittendorff, 13 July 1913.

The Piansecco Hut, a haven of peace.

The 'little Aiguille Noire de Peuterey', as mountaineers in the Val Bedretto like to call it, may not be as needle-like as its illustrious cousin on the flanks of Mont Blanc, but it is still a very shapely mountain. As for most of the other cliffs around the Piansecco Hut, the best known routes on the Poncione di Cassina Baggio face south. Nowadays, few teams do the full traverse of the South Ridge, as the popularity of climbs in the modern idiom has led to traditional routes such as this falling out of favour. For some, this is a shame; for others it offers the chance to enjoy the old classics in traditional solitude. In fact, one of the pleasures of climbing this jagged ridge is the feeling of going back to another era. On a bright autumn day, it may even seem like time has stood still. What is more, the moderate difficulties allow for a more relaxed approach, making it surprisingly easy to step down a gear and resist the rush that is so often part of summer mountaineering. Pleasant climbing on superb granite leads to an outstanding summit vista of the giants of the Bernese Oberland; at the end of a beautiful late season day, you may find it difficult to turn away from such an exquisite view.

# TESSIN ALPS

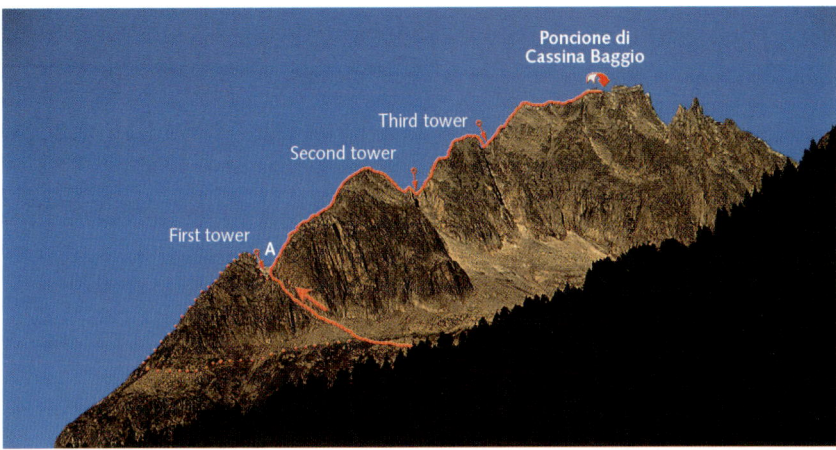

## APPROACH
Head west along the path from the Piansecco Hut to the Ri dell' Acqua. Go up the slopes on the left bank of the stream until above a line of cliffs. At around 2,360m, bear south to get to the ridge. As the abseil descent from the first tower (2,494m) is unpleasant (loose rock), it is best to start the climb at the notch between the first two towers (2,645m), reached by climbing an easy grassy gully.

## SOUTH RIDGE
The route along the ridge is quite obvious. Here are a few details. Climb the gendarme above the notch (2,616m) after the second tower (nice climbing). Do a 25m abseil down the west side of the ridge, beside a long slab. Descend from the third tower by a 20m abseil, then move back on to the crest after a section of walking (peg at the foot of a 3–4m-high wall). There is a red gendarme halfway between the third tower and the summit. 5m before this gendarme, climb down on the right (old peg).

## DESCENT
Go down the loose north face to the Chüebodengletscher. Head north-east to the Gerenpass, then descend south-east to the foot of the cliffs of the Poncione di Cassina Baggio. After a short distance, pick up the path (cairns), at first on the crest of a moraine, that leads back to Piansecco.

Lovely climbing on magnificent granite.

# PIZZO DEL PRÉVAT (2,558m)

## NORTH-EAST RIDGE AND NORTH-EAST PILLAR

**ROAD ACCESS:** from the Valais, A9 motorway to *Sierre-est*, then cantonal road to Brig, Ulrichen, Nufenenpass, Airolo, A2 motorway to Quinto, then cantonal road to Rodi. From the south, A2 motorway to Quinto, then cantonal road to Rodi.
**START POINT:** Leit Hut, 2,257m (698'330/146'980). Tel: 091 8681920. 1½ hrs from the top of the Rodi–Lago Tremorgio gondola lift.
**DIFFICULTY:** AD+, 5a for the North-east Ridge. D+, 5c for the North-east Pillar. Exposed climbing on the pillar. Little *in situ* gear on the ridge. Alpine descent.
**TIMES:** approach 2 hrs; climbs 3 hrs for the ridge, 4 hrs for the pillar; descent 45 mins–1 hr.
**VERTICAL HEIGHT:** 720m from Lago Tremorgio.
**CONDITIONS:** dry rock – lichen on the rock becomes slippery in damp conditions.
**SPECIFIC GEAR:** 50m single rope. For the ridge: set of nuts, small and medium cams, six quickdraws. For the pillar: rock shoes, ten quickdraws. Nuts and friends not needed.
**IN SITU GEAR:** a few bolts on the North-east Ridge. No *in situ* belays. The North-east Pillar is fully bolted.
**MAP:** 1252 Ambri-Piotta.
**FIRST ASCENTS:** North-east Ridge: unknown.
North-east Pillar: U. Bernasconi, A. Magistri & R. Rovagnati, 18 July 1943.

Pizzo del Prévat is a very popular venue, so it is rare to have a climb here to yourself. This is particularly true of the North-east Ridge, which receives several ascents every fine summer's day, making it one of the most popular routes in the Tessin Alps. Combining lovely climbing on perfect rock with impeccable gear and a relatively short approach, what more could you ask for? Fewer people, perhaps. But at least there is minimal danger from stone fall, even if there are several parties on the route. The best option is to come here midweek, although there are plenty of other routes to choose from should the ridge be too crowded.

Teams wanting to get the best value from their visit can easily do both of the routes described here on the same day. In this case, it is best to start by climbing the North-east Ridge in 'big boots', followed by the North-east Pillar in rock shoes as the icing on the cake. But don't forget to take your boots for the descent. A final detail: the truly magnificent setting ensures that the pleasures of climbing here are as aesthetic as they are physical.

### APPROACH

From the top of the gondola, follow the path round the eastern shore of Lago Tremorgio. Go across the Alpe di Campolungo (2,086m) to the Passo Campolungo (2,318m). Traverse across the scree below the north face of the Pizzo del Prévat (path, cairns) and go up to the foot of the North-east Ridge or the North-east Pillar, which are about 50m apart.

### NORTH-EAST RIDGE

Avoid the first few metres of the ridge by moving on to it from the left (path). Follow the crest of the ridge to below the final, more difficult wall (the line is obvious). Head left across grass to belay in a notch at the foot of this wall. Several lines can be climbed to get to the summit, but some of the nicest climbing is in the middle of the wall (nut and cam protection).

### NORTH-EAST PILLAR

P1: Nice 5b/5b+ pitch (intermediary belay if you want to start higher up).
P2: Move left then come back on to the crest. 4c.
P3: 5b, belay on a large terrace.
P4: Go up to the first bolt, then bear left. Short, exposed descent, then follow the crest. 5b.

# TESSIN ALPS

**P5:** Outstanding pitch on the crest of the pillar. Bold 5c.

The upper section can be climbed in several places. There are no *in situ* belays, but the climbing is never difficult (5c at first but easing to grade 3) and always very pleasant. Exiting on to the summit from the right allows you to make the best of the climbing right to the end.

## DESCENT

Follow the path down the south-east ridge to the first abseil (15m), which can be avoided by some easy down climbing. Continue down the exposed path. Two 15m abseils. Climb down to the notch at the foot of the ridge. Follow the path back to the start of the routes.

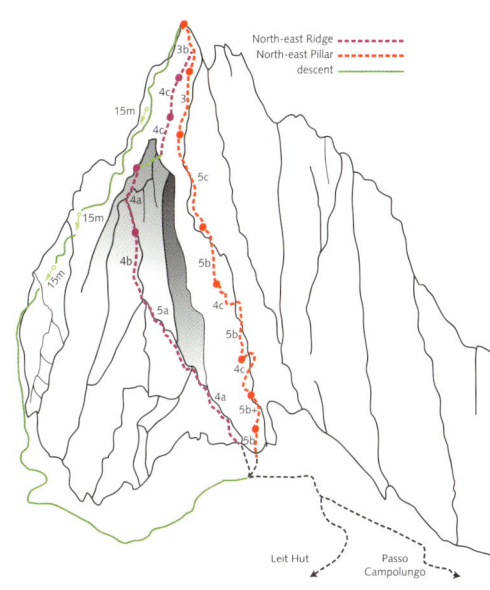

# PIZ CAVARDIRAS (2,948m)

## SOUTH RIDGE

**ROAD ACCESS:** from the Valais, A9 motorway to *Sierre-est*, then cantonal road to Brig, Furkapass, Oberalppass, Disentis. From the Tessin, A2 motorway to Göschenen, then cantonal road to Andermatt, Oberalppass, Disentis. From the north, A2 motorway to Lucerne, Altdorf, Göschenen, then as above.
**START POINT:** the route can be done in a day from the top of the Disentis-Caischavedra cable car.
**DIFFICULTY:** D, 4+ (one pitch of 5+ or A0). The route is long, so it is essential to climb efficiently and not waste time.
**TIMES:** approach 3¼ hrs; climb 4-5 hrs; descent 3½-4 hrs. It is best to bivouac near the Caischavedra cable car station.
**VERTICAL HEIGHT:** 1,320m.
**CONDITIONS:** dry rock. Lichen makes the rock very slippery in damp conditions.
**SPECIFIC GEAR:** 50m single rope, rock shoes, eight quickdraws, medium and large nuts.
**IN SITU GEAR:** the addition of new bolts has given the route a new lease of life. *In situ* belays.
**MAP:** 1212 Amsteg.
**FIRST ASCENT:** H. Bernhard & P. Condrau, 1949.

This minor summit in the Grisons may not be as striking as some of its neighbours, but it is a little gem. What is more, perseverance is needed to appreciate its charms, as the first part of the South Ridge is nothing special. Your reward comes in the middle section of the route, which includes a series of excellent pitches as well as the hardest climbing. The difficulties ease again just below the summit, giving you the freedom to soak up the exceptional view. To the north, huge limestone walls fade into the distance; to the east, the imposing mass of the Tödi – the monarch of the central Swiss Alps – dominates the horizon; to the west and a little closer, the glacial slopes of the Oberalpstock are just calling out to be skied. The views to the south are less dramatic, but the giants of the Valais and Bernese Oberland can be made out in the distance. Will you be able to recognise them? In these heights there reigns a tranquillity not to be found on every summit in the Alps, allowing you to savour a few precious hours of peaceful reverie during both the approach and the descent.

The Oberalpstock dominates the horizon during the descent to the Brunnipass.

# GRISON ALPS

## 26

Just before the summit.

# PIZ CAVARDIRAS
## SOUTH RIDGE

### APPROACH
Follow the waymarked path from the Caischavedra cable car station (1,862m) to Lag Serein (2,073m). Continue towards the Brunnipass (2,721m) but turn off the path at around 2,540m and head east towards the cliffs of Piz Cavardiras (scree, a few cairns along the path). Climb the rocks on the right bank of an unpleasant-looking gully to get to the foot of the South Ridge.

### SOUTH RIDGE
Go straight up slabs and a chimney (3+). Continue up the grassy rocks above the belay, then move right on to the ridge. The first few metres of the ridge are horizontal and consist of a series of teeth.

*More lovely rock.*

From the belay at the foot of one of the first teeth, move on to the east face. A delicate step down (grade 4, *in situ* sling) leads to a notch. The next few difficulties are turned on the left (another step down protected by an *in situ* sling). Abseil to a notch at the foot of a distinctive tower. Climb the tower (3), exiting left just before the top. Abseil down. The climbing improves over the next three pitches (3, 4+, 3), which lead to the two crux pitches. The *in situ* gear facilitates route finding. Two excellent, well-protected pitches (4+ and 5+/A0) mark the end of the difficulties. At the top of the second pitch, go past the bolt and peg belay just before the top of the wall on the right to a comfortable belay (two bolts) on the crest a few metres higher. Climb an off-putting wall (5+/A0) and gain a platform from where a final abseil leads to the foot of the summit step.

Follow the *in situ* slings. Approximately 10m after the only bolt in the first pitch (3), exit left to get to the belay. Move back on to the crest and follow it to the summit (3+, 2).

### DESCENT
Follow the ridge linking Piz Cavardiras to its north-western neighbour, the Brichlig (2,964m). Go just below the right-hand side of its summit then move on to the south-west ridge (cable) and follow it until it flattens out.

A belay/abseil station on the crest marks the start of the descent down the south face. Climb easily down the south face for a few metres to get to another abseil station. From here, four 20–25m abseils lead to a large and easily visible scree-covered ledge. Follow the line of bolts and abseil from the bolt belays. Traverse along the horizontal band of scree to its western end without descending too far, then move back on to the westward-trending ridge. Easily gain the Brunnipass and follow the waymarked trail back to the cable car.

# GRISON ALPS

# PIZ BALZET (2,869m)

## SOUTH RIDGE

**ROAD ACCESS:** from the north, A1 motorway to Zurich, A3 then A13 past Chur to Thusis. Then Tiefencastel, Julierpass, Maloja, Pranzaira. From the Valais, A9 motorway to *Sierre-est*, then cantonal road to Brig, Furkapass, Oberalppass and Bonaduz to Thusis, then as above. From the south, Lecco in Italy, Chiavenna, Pranzaira.
**START POINT:** Albigna Hut, 2,333m (770'660/133'360). Tel: 081 8221405. 45 mins from the top of the Pranzaira–Lägh da l'Albigna gondola lift.
**DIFFICULTY:** D, 4c. A relatively short route, but demands efficient ropework to avoid wasting time.
**TIMES:** approach 1 hr; climb 3½ hrs; descent 1½ hrs.
**VERTICAL HEIGHT:** 550m.
**CONDITIONS:** dry rock. Comes into condition quickly after bad weather.
**SPECIFIC GEAR:** 50m rope, eight quickdraws, small and medium cams, rock shoes.
**IN SITU GEAR:** bolts, *in situ* abseil stations for the descent.
**MAPS:** 1276 Val Bregaglia, 1296 Sciora.
**FIRST ASCENT:** Walter Risch, solo, 1922.

The Albigna basin contains a huge number of rock climbs covering all tastes, from massive expeditions that leave you exhausted (and which are rarely climbed for that very reason) to short technical climbs with negligible walk-ins. Between these two extremes, a huge number of routes of all styles has given Albigna an enviable reputation. Piz Balzet epitomises this diversity, as long routes with little fixed gear rub shoulders with less committing climbs. However, the Bregalia is justifiably known for its minimal bolting, so most of the area's routes require a rack of cams and nuts, in addition to quickdraws. Quite deservedly, the South Ridge of Piz Balzet is one of Albigna's most classic routes. The approach does not require a superhuman effort, the line is obvious, the *in situ* gear has been placed intelligently and the descent poses no major problems. What is more, the rock does nothing to tarnish the Bregalia's reputation. And, if you are lucky enough to do the route on a clear day, you should be able to recognise the most famous peaks of the Valais and Oberland, off in the distance.

### APPROACH

From the hut, head north-east up the path to the Pass da Casnil. At the small plateau at around 2,600m, to the east of Piz dal Pal, head due north towards Piz Balzet. A path leads to the foot of the route, to the left of the large gully that comes down from the summit. Start to the left of a jammed block.

### SOUTH RIDGE

**P1:** Climb straight up. 4c, then 3c towards the top. Belay in a chimney.
**P2:** Go right round the roof. 3a.
**P3:** Easy. 2c. P2 and P3 can be climbed as one pitch. Belay (two bolts) below a roof.

P8: what to wear, boots or rock shoes?

# GRISON ALPS

P4: Go over the roof and belay on a large ledge. 3c.
P5: System of parallel cracks. Good holds on the wall on the right. 4a. Easier variant on the left. 3c.
P6: Lovely climbing on the crest. 4a.
P7: Easy at first, then short wall on the rounded crest. Walk up to belay below a slab.
P8: Crux: a 4c slab, bolts. Go left round a roof, then move up on to flatter ground (crack at the back).

Summit ridge: easy start followed by a short wall (3c, two variants) and then easy again.

## DESCENT

Go down the east ridge to the first abseil station (25m), a few metres below the crest on the right. Continue following scuff marks and cairns. At a wide notch in the ridge, move on to the north face to go round a tower (cairns), staying at more or less the same height. Ignore the abseil slings and descend another 5m to do a 25m abseil from a chain belay. Move back on to the south face at the next notch, then walk down the left bank of the gully for about 50m. A final 25m abseil leads to the scree slope. Follow cairns and a path back to the hut.

# PUNTA DA L'ALBIGNA (2,825m)

## MEULI ROUTE
**ROAD ACCESS:** see route no.27 (page 86).
**START POINT:** see route no.27 (page 86).
**DIFFICULTY:** D, one pitch 5a+. Several grade-4 pitches. Route finding not always obvious, despite the *in situ* gear. Possible to do just the first 10 pitches.
**TIMES:** approach 30 mins; climb 6 hrs; descent 2 hrs.
**VERTICAL HEIGHT:** 580m.
**CONDITIONS:** dry rock. Wait until the afternoon to get some sun.
**SPECIFIC GEAR:** 50m single rope, ten quickdraws, rock shoes.
**IN SITU GEAR:** bolts.
**MAPS:** 1276 Val Bregaglia, 1296 Sciora.
**FIRST ASCENT:** Konrad Freund, Hans Gschwend & Conradin Meuli, 16 September 1961.

Punta da l'Albigna rises proudly above its eponymous lake. It is one of the few peaks in the area, alongside Piz dal Päl and Piz Balzet, not on the ridgeline surrounding the reservoir. This little beauty prefers to display her charms closer to the Albigna Hut. And it must be said, when her flanks burn golden in the afternoon sun, it is difficult to tear your eyes away. Several excellent routes have been climbed on the north-west face of Point 2,653m.

The initial pitches climb a highly featured slab.

The Meuli Route was first climbed in 1961 and quickly became one of the area's great classics. With its superbly featured granite and modern bolts added in 2002, it is likely to retain that status for many years to come. A wonderful route on its own, the Meuli can be extended by climbing the north-west ridge of the summit tower to produce a very long and superbly varied outing. Wait until the afternoon, when the sun comes on to the face, and you are sure to have a great day. Although it is in the heart of the mountains, Albigna has a slightly Mediterranean ambiance that is highly conducive to lounging in the sun. Be careful you don't get so distracted you miss out on the wonderful climbing!

### APPROACH
Follow the path south from the hut towards the reservoir. At the pipeline, contour round leftwards to the foot of the route (path). The climb starts at a corner formed by the angle between two large areas of slabs ('Moderne Zeiten' written just to the left on the slabs).

### MEULI ROUTE
**P1:** Wide corner. Belay after 30m shared with *Moderne Zeiten*, which then heads right. 4a.
**P2:** End of the corner. 4b.
**P3:** Straight up the chimney on the left. Move back left from the bolt on the wall. 3c.
**P4:** Stepped ledges. 3c.
**P5** and **P6:** Slabs. Easy to get lost. Aim for the corner on the left. 3c.

# GRISON ALPS  28

Punta da l'Albigna

# PUNTA DA L'ALBIGNA
## MEULI ROUTE

**P7:** Corner. Exit left at the top, one peg (bold climbing). 4b.
**P8:** Slabs to get back on the crest to the left. 3b.
**P9:** Ramp on the right with no bolts, then chimney with one peg. At two bolts (one bent), head right to gain another belay 10m higher (a little rope drag but more comfortable belay). 4b.
**P10:** Slabs. 4a.

Transition to the summit tower: Follow an obvious gully on the left to get to a large, scree-filled bowl. Go up the right-hand side of the bowl (cairns) to a bottleneck at the foot of the north-west ridge of Punta da l'Albigna. Traverse across a small gully and start climbing again at a bolted slab.
**P11:** Follow the right-hand variant (well protected) along a diagonal crack. 5a+.
**P12:** Keep 1–2m to the right of the crest. Belay 5–6m from the crest. 4a.
**P13–P16:** 3b/c. Start by climbing the crest, then follow a ramp. A few pegs. Some thread belays.

### DESCENT
Go along the summit ridge to the south summit. Do a 25m abseil to a large ledge on the south face. Continue behind a block, where a cable leads to a second 25m abseil. Go up a path to a saddle to the east, then cross into the rocky combe to the north. Follow the cairns and a discontinuous path to the stream draining the Vadrec dal Cantun. Cross the stream (it may be necessary to wade across if the stream is high) and continue past the pipeline back to the hut.

P11: follow the crack ...

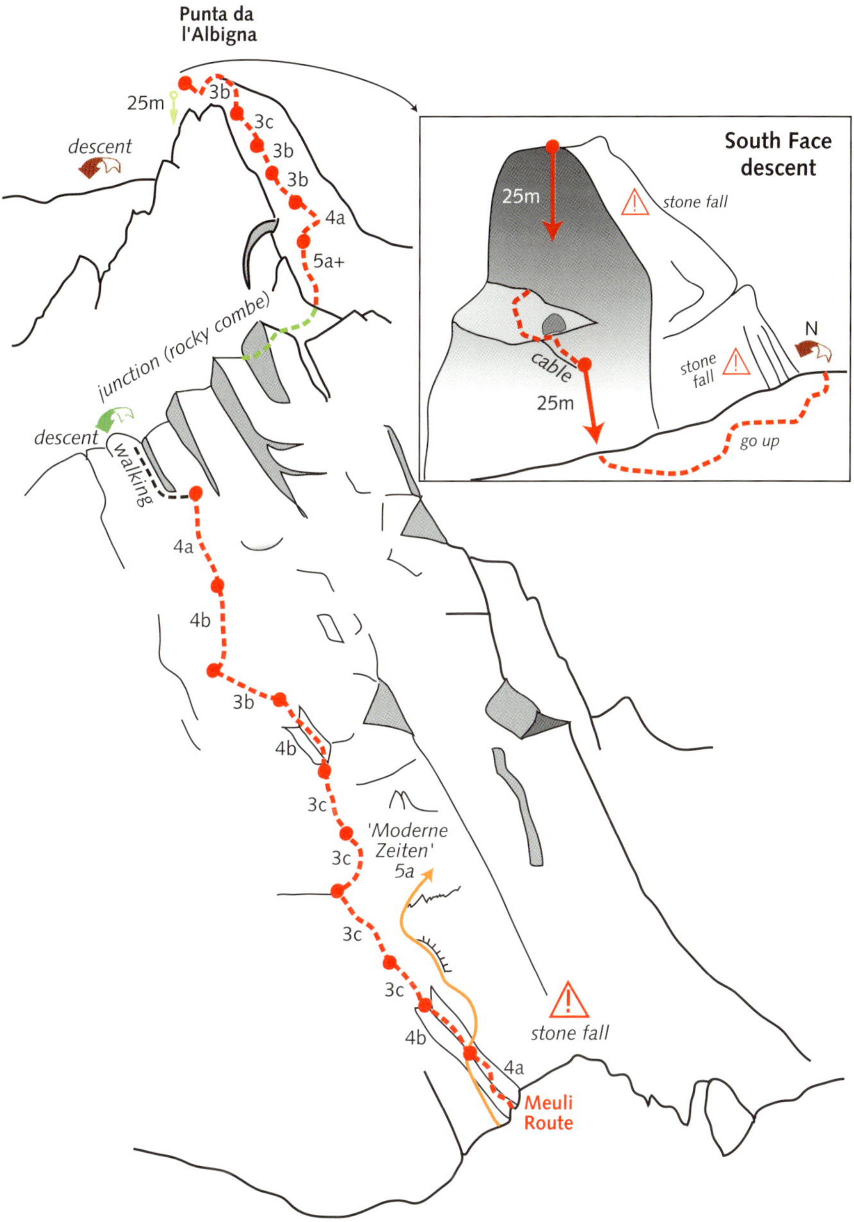
Punta da l'Albigna
25m
descent
3b
3c
3b
3b
4a
5a+
junction (rocky combe)
descent
walking
4a
4b
3b
4b
3c
3c
'Moderne Zeiten' 5a
3c
3c
4b
4a
stone fall
Meuli Route
South Face descent
25m
stone fall
cable
25m
stone fall
N
go up

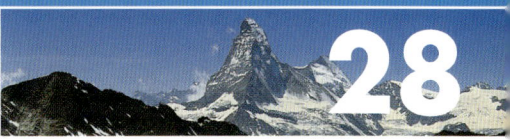

# PIZ KESCH (3,417m)

## NORTH-EAST RIDGE OF THE KESCHNADEL AND KESCHGRAT

**ROAD ACCESS:** from the north, A1 motorway to Zurich, A3 then A13 past Chur to Thusis. From Thusis, go through Tiefencastel, Filisur, Albulapass. From the Valais, A9 motorway to *Sierre-est*, then cantonal road to Brig, Furkapass, Oberalppass and Bonaduz to Thusis, then as above.
**START POINT:** Es-scha Hut, 2,594m (788'750/165'200). Tel: 081 8541755. 1¾ hrs from Punt Granda (spot height 2,251m on the Albulapass road, approx. 2.5 km east of the pass), via La Fuorcla Gualdauna.
**DIFFICULTY:** AD+, 4. One or two difficult sections. Complex route finding on the descent from Piz Kesch.
**TIMES:** approach 2 hrs; climb 4 hrs; descent 2 hrs.
**VERTICAL HEIGHT:** 950m.
**CONDITIONS:** dry rock. Snow on the Keschnadel can make some sections more difficult. Snow is less of a problem on the Keschgrat.
**SPECIFIC GEAR:** 50m rope, small and medium cams, six quickdraws.
**IN SITU GEAR:** a few bolts on the North-east Ridge of the Keschnadel. *In situ* belays.
**MAP:** 1237 Albulapass.
**FIRST ASCENTS:** Keschnadel: M. & P. Schucan, 29 July 1906.
Keschgrat: Paul Güssfeld with Hans Grass, 28 September 1877.

Piz Kesch occupies an enviable position among the summits of the Upper Engadine. Rising higher than all the surrounding peaks, it has a superb view of the icy summits of the Bernina. When the first rays of the sun softly illuminate the landscape, as at the dawn of time, it is easy to appreciate how lucky you are to be here. Of course, there are other mountains in the area from which you can admire this spectacle, but none of them has such great climbs as Piz Kesch. The fantastic North-east Ridge of the Keschnadel (Aguoglia d'Es-cha in Romansh) followed by the traverse of the Keschgrat to the summit are worth coming for on their own.

The beauty of this corner of the Grisons, the relatively small number of climbers at the Es-cha Hut and the picturesque village of Bergün on the beautiful road to the Albulapass, all contribute to the pleasure of climbing here. And, on top of all that, the north face of Piz Kesch still has a glacier worthy of the name, something that has become quite rare in this part of the Alps.

### APPROACH

Follow the path from the hut to the Porta d'Es-cha (3,008m, blue and white waymarkers). Head south-west across the glacier to the saddle at the foot of the Keschnadel.

The Bernina range provides a spectacular backdrop.

# GRISON ALPS

**29**

## NORTH-EAST RIDGE OF THE KESCHNADEL

Start on the easy south side of the ridge. Follow the crest past a shoulder to the foot of the first step, which is climbed directly (4, nice climbing). Easy slabs lead to the second step. Go up leftwards, then move back right on to the crest (4a). Go up slabs to the third step (3), which is avoided by traversing horizontally right for 30m (often snow covered, belay at the foot of the wall). Head back diagonally left on the edge of a chimney to regain the crest (4a), which leads to a slot followed by an exposed slab. Fall across the slot to place your hands on the slab, then move your feet up. Go straight up a crack (4, crux, three bolts), then continue to the summit (3c).

## PIZ KESCH, TRAVERSE OF THE KESCHGRAT

Descend the north side of the summit for 10m, then head diagonally left (cairn). Follow a narrow ledge and a gully to the western foot of the Keschnadel (abseil possible). The central summit (3,405m) is reached easily by heading left round a small step. Descend into a notch, and then a second, larger notch (down-climbing, lots of holds, small overhang at the bottom). A pinnacle on the route can be turned on either side, with the easiest line depending on conditions.

Storming the citadel.

From the deepest depression on the ridge, go up to a gendarme and climb it via the ridge and then a ledge on the east face. Continue to a belay. 10m abseil. Go up easily to the summit.

## DESCENT

The descent goes down the east face and north-east ridge of Piz Kesch. The route is well trodden but the rock is loose, so take care if there are other teams above or below you. Begin by descending eastwards, then keep close to the ridge on the left. Move back on to the east face for the middle third, then head diagonally leftwards to a wide shoulder on the north-east ridge. Go more or less straight down to the glacier.

# PIZ BERNINA (4,049m)

## BIANCOGRAT

**ROAD ACCESS:** from the north, A1 motorway to Zurich, A3 then A13 past Chur to Thusis. From Thusis, go through Tiefencastel, Julierpass and Saint Moritz to Pontresina. From the Valais, A9 motorway to *Sierre-est*, then cantonal road to Brig, Furkapass, Oberalppass and Bonaduz to Thusis, then as above. From the south, Lecco in Italy, Sondrio, Tirano, Passo del Bernina, Pontresina.
**START POINT:** Tschierva Hut, 2,583m (787'720/142'090). Tel: 081 8426391. 3½ hrs from Pontresina via the Val Roseg.
**DIFFICULTY:** AD, grade-3 rock, 45° snow, a long mixed route.
**TIMES:** approach 3 hrs; climb 3–5 hrs; descent 1½ hrs. Allow 5½–6 hrs the next day for the descent to Morteratsch.
**VERTICAL HEIGHT:** 1,500m.
**CONDITIONS:** dry rock but snow on the Biancograt. Conditions are generally best in July. At the end of the season, there are often areas of bare ice and stone fall is more frequent.
**SPECIFIC GEAR:** 30m rope, crampons, ice axe, four quickdraws, three or four ice screws.
**IN SITU GEAR:** cat's eyes along the approach path, pegs, bolts.
**MAPS:** 1257 St. Moritz, 1277 Piz Bernina.
**FIRST ASCENT:** Carl Colmus with Chasper Grass the elder & Ulrich Grass, 12 August 1878.

The Biancograt, or Crast'Alva in Romansh, the local language, is undoubtedly the most famous snow climb in the eastern Alps. It is as simple as a child's pencil line and as elegant as the sinuous curves of a dancer. Few perspectives in the mountains are so fluid: viewed from a neighbouring summit, the Biancograt appears to shimmer in the wind. It sometimes appears as if the mere presence of climbers treading its long crest could throw its harmonious oscillations out of sync. Thus, the Biancograt casts its spell, although the charm is more powerful from a distance than when you are engrossed in the climbing. Oh, climbing this legendary ridge is by no means a chore and you are always aware of being on an exceptional route, but you almost forget the splendour of your surroundings: Piz Palü, Piz Roseg, Piz Scerscen, the vast glaciers. Here, more than elsewhere, just contemplating the magical line can suffice.

Some mountaineers descend from the top of Pizzo Bianco at almost 4,000m, where the snow ends, as going on means an extremely long descent back to Morteratsch. If you have the time, rather than rushing to finish the route the same day, a much better option is to continue over the summit of the Bernina and spend the night at the Marco e Rosa Hut (3,597m, tel: +39 0342 515370), just below. Descending the next day, you will have the time to truly enjoy the magnificent scenery.

### APPROACH

From the hut, follow the path south-east above the Vadret da Tschierva. After the path disappears in the scree slopes, the route is marked by cairns and cat's eyes. Move on to the glacier at around 2,950m

Alone in the world ...

# GRISON ALPS

**30**

Battered by the wind, the snowy crest of the Biancograt clings valiantly to the crystalline rocks of the Bernina.

# PIZ BERNINA
## BIANCOGRAT

and go up its right bank. Head left into the glacial combe at the foot of Piz Prievlus and climb a steep snowfield to the Fuorcla Prievlusa (3,430m). If there is not enough snow or if there are teams above you, it is better to gain the saddle by going up the rocks of Piz Prievlus (metal bars), just to the north.

### BIANCOGRAT
Start on the western side of the ridge (3, pegs, bolts), then move left on to the crest. Move on to the east side before the end of the rock section in order to join the snow at the foot of the Biancograt proper (if the snowy traverse is not in condition, continue to the summit and then descend a short distance). Follow the snowy ridge to Pizzo Bianco (or Piz Palü, 3,995m). Continue along the eastern side of the now rocky crest until you are above a notch. Climb down to the *in situ* belay and abseil (15m) into the notch. Climb the next tower or avoid it on the right. Continue to the summit of the Bernina.

### DESCENT TO THE MARCO E ROSA HUT
Go down the south ridge (rock then snow) to La Spedla (4,020m). Continue along the south-east ridge (snow, grade-2 rock, pegs). At around 3,850m, either head down the south face or continue to the end of the ridge (3, pegs, safer). Head south down easy snow slopes to the Marco e Rosa Hut (3,597m).

### DESCENT TO MORTERATSCH
From the hut, traverse east across the glacier and below the Bellavista Ridge to just before the Fuorcla Bellavista (3,688m). Head north down the snowy spur to spot height 3,482m, above Fortezza. Continue to Fortezza (3,372m, orange paint marks, abseil or climb down), then follow the crest of the ridge to spot height 3,186m. Go down the rock to the Vadret da la Fortezza. Continue down the right bank of the glacier, then descend the scree slopes of Isla Persa. Follow the path west to the confluence of the Vadret Pers and the Vadret de la Morteratsch. Go down the median moraine past the glacier tongue to the path to Morteratsch.

---

The routes included in this guidebook are presented for information only. Every mountaineer is responsible for his or her own decisions. Choices must take into account one's abilities and the risks arising from the conditions in the mountains. The route descriptions are accurate for the conditions and date on which they were climbed; however, climbers should check that a chosen route has not changed in any way, for example, due to rock-fall, glacial retreat or removal of *in situ* gear. The authors, editors and publishers cannot be held responsible for any accidents that occur on any of the routes described in this guidebook. As the guidebook is not updated at frequent intervals, it cannot be considered expert testimony in a court of law.

#### SAFETY STATEMENT
Climbing and mountaineering are activities that carry a risk of personal injury or death. Participants must be aware of and accept that these risks are present and they should be responsible for their own actions and involvement. Nobody involved in the writing and production of this guidebook accepts any responsibility for any errors that it contains, nor are they liable for any injuries or damage that may arise from its use. Climbing and mountaineering are inherently dangerous and the fact that individual descriptions in this volume do not point out such dangers does not mean that they do not exist. Take care.